The Crisis In Russia...

Arthur Ransome

THE CRISIS IN RUSSIA

BY
ARTHUR RANSOME
Author of "Russia in 1919"

NEW YORK B. W. HUEBSCH, INC. MCMXXI

ENGLISH 1

TO
WILLIAM PETERS
OF ABERDEEN

INTRODUCTION

THE characteristic of a revolutionary country is that change is a quicker process there than elsewhere. As the revolution recedes into the past the process of change slackens speed. Russia is no longer the dizzying kaleidoscope that it was in 1917. No longer does it change visibly from week to week as it changed in 1918. Already, to get a clear vision of the direction in which it is changing, it is necessary to visit it at intervals of six months, and quite useless to tap the political barometer several times a day as once upon a time one used to do. . . . But it is still changing very fast. My journal of "Russia in 1919," while giving as I believe a fairly accurate picture of the state of affairs in February and March of 1919, pictures a very different stage in the development of the revolution from that which would be found by observers to-day.

The prolonged state of crisis in which the country has been kept by external war, while strengthening the ruling party by rallying even their enemies to their support, has had the other effects that a national crisis always has on the internal politics of a country. Methods of government which in normal times would no doubt be softened or disguised by ceremonial usage are used nakedly and justified by necessity. We have seen the same thing in belligerent and non-revolutionary countries, and, for the impartial student, it has been interesting to observe that, when this test of crisis is applied, the actual governmental machine in every country looks very much like that in every other. They wave different flags to stimulate enthusiasm and to justify submission. But that is all. Under the stress of war, "constitutional safeguards" go by the board "for the public good," in Moscow as elsewhere. Under that stress it becomes clear that, in spite of its novel constitution, Russia is governed much as other countries are governed, the real directive power lying in the hands of a comparatively small body which is able by hook or crook to infect with its conscious will a population largely indifferent and inert. A visitor to Moscow to-day would find much of the constitutional machinery that was in full working order in the spring of 1919 now falling into rust and disrepair. He would not be able once a week or so to attend a meeting of the All-Russian Executive and hear discussions in this parliament of the questions of the day. No one tries to shirk the fact that the Executive Committee has fallen into desuetude, from which, when the stress slackens enough to permit ceremonial that has not an immediate agitational value, it may some day be revived. The bulk of its members have been at the front or here and there about the country wrestling with the economic problem, and their work is more useful than their chatter. Thus brutally is the thing stated. The continued stress has made the muscles, the actual works, of the revolution more visible than formerly. The working of the machine is not only seen more clearly, but is also more frankly stated (perhaps simply because they too see it now more clearly), by the leaders themselves.

I want in this book to describe the working of the machine as I now see it. But it is not only the machine which is more nakedly visible than it was. The stress to which it is being subjected has also not so much changed its character as become easier of analysis. At least, I seem to myself to see it differently. In the earlier days it seemed quite simply the struggle between a revolutionary and non-revolutionary countries. I now think that that struggle is a foolish, unnecessary, lunatic incident which disguised from us the existence of a far more serious struggle, in which the revolutionary and non-revolutionary governments are fighting on the same side. They fight without coöperation, and throw insults and bullets at each other in the middle of the struggle, but they are fighting for the same thing. They are fighting the same enemy. Their quarrel with each other is for both parties merely a harassing accompaniment of the struggle to which all Europe is committed, for the salvage of what is left of European civilization.

The threat of a complete collapse of civilization is more imminent in Russia than elsewhere. But it is clear enough in Poland, it cannot be disregarded in Germany, there is no doubt of its existence in Italy, France is conscious of it; it is only in England and America that this threat is not among the waking nightmares of everybody. Unless the struggle, which has hitherto been going against us, takes a turn for the better, we shall presently be quite unable to ignore it ourselves.

I have tried to state the position in Russia today: on the one hand to describe the crisis itself, the threat which is forcing these people to an extreme of effort, and on the other hand to describe the organization that is facing that threat; on the one hand to set down what are the main characteristics of the crisis, on the other hand to show how the comparatively small body of persons actually supplying the Russian people with its directives set about the stupendous task of moving that vast inert mass, not along the path of least resistance, but along a path which, while alike unpleasant and extremely difficult, does seem to them to promise some sort of eventual escape.

No book is entirely objective, so I do not in the least mind stating my own reason for writing this one (which has taken time that I should have liked to spend on other and very different things). Knowledge of this reason will permit the reader to make allowances for such bias as I have been unable to avoid, and so, by judicious reading, to make my book perhaps nearly as objective as I should myself wish it to be.

It has been said that when two armies face each other across a battle front and engage in mutual slaughter, they may be considered as a single army engaged in suicide. Now it seems to me that when countries, each one severally doing its best to arrest its private economic ruin, do their utmost to accelerate the economic ruin of each other, we are witnessing something very like the suicide of civilization itself. There are people in both camps who believe that armed and economic conflict between revolutionary and non-revolutionary Europe, or if you like between Capitalism and Communism, is inevitable. These people, in both camps, are doing their best to make it inevitable. Sturdy pessimists, in Moscow no less than in London and Paris, they go so far as to say "the sooner the better," and by all means in their power try to precipitate a conflict. Now the main effort in Russia to-day, the struggle which absorbs the chief attention of all but the few Communist Churchills and Communist Millcrands who, blind to all else, demand an immediate pitched battle over the prostrate body of civilization, is directed to finding a way for Russia herself out of the crisis, the severity of which can hardly be realized by people who have not visited the country again and again, and to bringing her as quickly as possible into a state in which she can export her raw materials and import the manufactured goods of which she stands in need. I believe that this struggle is ours as well as Russia's, though we to whom the threat is less imminent, are less desperately engaged. Victory or defeat in this struggle in Russia, or anywhere else on the world's surface, is victory or defeat for every one. The purpose of my book is to make that clear. For, bearing that in mind, I cannot but think that every honest man, of whatever party, who cares more for humanity than for politics, must do his utmost to postpone the conflict which a few extremists on each side of the barricades so fanatically desire. If that conflict is indeed inevitable, its consequences will be less devastating to a Europe cured of her wounds than to a Europe scarcely, even by the most hopeful, to be described as convalescent. But the conflict

may not be inevitable after all. No man not pur-
blind but sees that Communist Europe is changing no less than Capitalist Europe. If we succeed in postponing the struggle long enough, we
may well succeed in postponing it until the war-
like on both sides look in vain for the reasons of
their bellicosity.

CONTENTS

*** I am indebted to the Editor of the " Manchester Guardian " for permission to make use in some of the chapters of this book of material which has appeared in his paper.

[XV]

THE CRISIS IN RUSSIA

THE SHORTAGE OF THINGS

NOTHING can be more futile than to describe conditions in Russia as a sort of divine punishment
for revolution, or indeed to describe them at all
without emphasizing the fact that the crisis in
Russia is part of the crisis in Europe, and has been
in the main brought about like the revolution itself, by the same forces that have caused, for example, the crisis in Germany or the crisis in Austria.

No country in Europe is capable of complete
economic independence. In spite of her huge variety of natural resources, the Russian organism
seemed in 1914 to have been built up on the gen-
erous assumption that with Europe at least the
country was to be permanently at peace, or at the
most to engage in military squabbles which could
be reckoned in months, and would keep up the

prestige of the autocracy without seriously hampering imports and exports. Almost every country in Europe, with the exception of England, was better fitted to stand alone, was less completely specialized in a single branch of production. England, fortunately for herself, was not isolated during the war, and will not become isolated unless the development of the crisis abroad deprives her of her markets. England produces practically no food, but great quantities of coal, steel and manufactured goods. Isolate her absolutely, and she will not only starve, but will stop producing manufactured goods, steel and coal, because those who usually produce these things will be getting nothing for their labor except money which they will be unable to use to buy dinners, because there will be no dinners to buy. That supposititious case is a precise parallel to what has happened in Russia. Russia produced practically no manufactured goods (70 per cent. of her machinery she received from abroad), but great quantities of food. The blockade isolated her. By the blockade I do not mean merely the childish stupidity committed by ourselves, but the blockade, steadily increasing in strictness, which began in August,

1914, and has been unnecessarily prolonged by our stupidity. The war, even while for Russia it was not nominally a blockade, was so actually. The use of tonnage was perforce restricted to the transport of the necessaries of war, and these were narrowly defined as shells, guns and so on, things which do not tend to improve a country economically, but rather the reverse. The imports from Sweden through Finland were no sort of makeweight for the loss of Poland and Germany.

The war meant that Russia's ordinary imports practically ceased. It meant a strain on Russia, comparable to that which would have been put on England if the German submarine campaign had succeeded in putting an end to our imports of food from the Americas. From the moment of the Declaration of War, Russia was in the position of one "holding out," of a city standing a siege without a water supply, for her imports were so necessary to her economy that they may justly be considered as essential irrigation. There could be no question for her of improvement, of strengthening. She was faced with the fact until the war should end she had to do with what she had, and that the things she had formerly counted on importing would be replaced by guns and shells, to be used, as it turned out, in battering Russian property that happened to be in enemy hands. She even learned that she had to develop gun-making and shell-making at home, at the expense of those other industries which to some small extent might have helped her to keep going. And, just as in England such a state of affairs would lead to a cessation of the output of iron and coal in which England is rich, so in Russia, in spite of her corn lands, it led to a shortage of food.

The Russian peasant formerly produced food for which he was paid in money. With that money, formerly, he was able to clothe himself, to buy the tools of his labor, and further, though no doubt he never observed the fact, to pay for the engines and wagons that took his food to market. A huge percentage of the clothes and the tools and the engines and the wagons and the rails came from abroad, and even those factories in Russia which were capable of producing such things were, in many essentials, themselves dependent upon imports. Russian towns began to be hungry in 1915. In October of that year the Empress reported to the Emperor that the shrewd Rasputin had seen in a vision that it was necessary to bring wagons with flour, butter and sugar from Siberia, and proposed that for three days nothing else should be done. Then there would be no strikes. "He blesses you for the arrangement of these trains." In 1916 the peasants were burying their bread instead of bringing it to market. In the autumn of 1916 I remember telling certain most incredulous members of the English Government that there would be a most serious food shortage in Russia in the near future. In 1917 came the upheaval of the revolution, in 1918 peace, but for Russia, civil war and the continuance of the blockade. By July, 1919, the rarity of manufactured goods was such that it was possible two hundred miles south of Moscow to obtain ten eggs for a box of matches, and the rarity of goods requiring distant transport became such that in November, 1919, in Western Russia, the peasants would sell me nothing for money, whereas my neighbor in the train bought all he wanted in exchange for small quantities of salt.

It was not even as if, in vital matters, Russia

started the war in a satisfactory condition. The most vital of all questions in a country of huge distances must necessarily be that of transport. It is no exaggeration to say that only by fantastic efforts was Russian transport able to save its face and cover its worst deficiencies even before the war began. The extra strain put upon it by the transport of troops and the maintenance of the armies exposed its weakness, and with each succeeding week of war, although in 1916 and 1917 Russia did receive 775 locomotives from abroad, Russian transport went from bad to worse, making inevitable a creeping paralysis of Russian economic life, during the latter already acute stages of which the revolutionaries succeeded to the disease that had crippled their precursors.

In 1914 Russia had in all 20,057 locomotives, of which 15,047 burnt coal, 4,072 burnt oil and 938 wood. But that figure of twenty thousand was more impressive for a Government official, who had his own reasons for desiring to be impressed, than for a practical railway engineer, since of that number over five thousand engines were more than twenty years old, over two thousand were more than thirty years old, fifteen hundred were more than forty years old, and 147 patriarchs had passed their fiftieth birthday. Of the whole twenty thousand only 7,108 were under ten years of age. That was six years ago. In the meantime Russia has been able to make in quantities decreasing during the last five years by 40 and 50 per cent. annually, 2,990 new locomotives. In 1914 of the locomotives then in Russia about 17,000 were in working condition. In 1915 there were, in spite of 800 new ones, only 16,500. In 1916 the number of healthy locomotives was slightly higher, owing partly to the manufacture of 903 at home in the preceding year and partly to the arrival of 400 from abroad. In 1917 in spite of the arrival of a further small contingent the number sank to between 15,000 and 16,000. Early in 1918 the Germans in the Ukraine and elsewhere captured 3,000. Others were lost in the early stages of the civil war. The number of locomotives fell from 14,519 in January to 8,457 in April, after which the artificially instigated revolt of the Czecho-Slovaks made possible the fostering of civil war on a large scale, and the number fell swiftly to 4,679 in December. In 1919 the numbers varied less markedly, but the decline continued, and in December last year 4,141 engines were in working order. In January this year the number was 3,969, rising slightly in February, when the number was 4,019. A calculation was made before the war that in the best possible conditions the maximum Russian output of engines could be not more than 1,800 annually. At this rate in ten years the Russians could restore their collection of engines to something like adequate numbers. To-day, thirty years would be an inadequate estimate, for some factories, like the Votkinsky, have been purposely ruined by the Whites, in others the lathes and other machinery for building and repairing locomotives are worn out, many of the skilled engineers were killed in the war with Germany, many others in defending the revolution, and it will be long before it will be possible to restore to the workmen or to the factories the favorable material conditions of 1912–13. Thus the main fact in the present crisis is that Russia possesses one-fifth of the number of locomotives which in 1914 was just sufficient to maintain her railway system in a state of efficiency which to English observers at that time was a joke. For six years she has been unable to import the necessary machinery for making engines or repairing them. Further, coal and oil have been, until recently, cut off by the civil war. The coal mines are left, after the civil war, in such a condition that no considerable output may be expected from them in the near future. Thus, even those engines which exist have had their efficiency lessened by being adapted in a rough and ready manner for burning wood fuel instead of that for which they were designed.

Let us now examine the combined effect of ruined transport and the six years' blockade on Russian life in town and country. First of all was cut off the import of manufactured goods from abroad. That has had a cumulative effect completed, as it were, and rounded off by the breakdown of transport. By making it impossible to bring food, fuel and raw material to the factories, the wreck of transport makes it impossible for Russian industry to produce even that modicum which it contributed to the general supply of manufactured goods which the Russian peasant was accustomed to receive in exchange for his production of food. On the whole the peasant himself eats rather more than he did before the war. But he has no matches, no salt, no clothes, no boots, no tools. The Communists are trying to put an end to illiteracy in Russia, and in the villages the most frequent excuse for keeping children from school is a request to come and see them, when they will be found, as I have seen them myself, playing naked about the stove, without boots or anything but a shirt, if that, in which to go and learn to read and write. Clothes and such things as matches are, however, of less vital importance than tools, the lack of which is steadily reducing Russia's actual power of food production. Before the war Russia needed from abroad huge quantities of agricultural implements, not only machines, but simple things like axes, sickles, scythes. In 1915 her own production of these things had fallen to 15.1 per cent. of her already inadequate peace-time output. In 1917 it had fallen to 2.1 per cent. The Soviet Government is making efforts to raise it, and is planning new factories exclusively for the making of these things. But, with transport in such a condition, a new factory means merely a new demand for material and fuel which there are neither engines nor wagons to bring. Meanwhile, all over Russia, spades are worn out, men are plowing with burnt staves instead of with plowshares, scratching the surface of the ground, and instead of harrowing with a steel-spiked harrow of some weight, are brushing the ground with light constructions of wooden spikes bound together with wattles.

The actual agricultural productive powers of Russia are consequently sinking. But things are no better if we turn from the rye and corn lands to the forests. Saws are worn out. Axes are worn out. Even apart from that, the shortage of transport affects the production of wood fuel, lack of which reacts on transport and on the factories and so on in a circle from which nothing but a large import of engines and wagons will provide an outlet. Timber can be floated down the rivers. Yes, but it must be brought to the rivers. Surely horses can do that. Yes, but horses must be fed, and oats do not grow in the forests. For example, this spring (1920) the best organized timber production was in Perm Government. There sixteen thousand horses have been mobilized for the work, but further

27

development is impossible for lack of forage. A telegram bitterly reports, "Two trains of oats from Ekaterinburg are expected day by day. If the oats arrive in time a considerable success will be possible." And if the oats do not arrive in time? Besides, not horses alone require to be fed. The men who cut the wood cannot do it on empty stomachs. And again rises a cry for trains that do not arrive, for food that exists somewhere, but not in the forest where men work. The general effect of the wreck of transport on food is stated as follows: Less than 12 per cent. of the oats required, less than 5 per cent. of the bread and salt required for really efficient working, were brought to the forests. Nonetheless three times as much wood has been prepared as the available transport has removed.

The towns suffer from lack of transport, and from the combined effect on the country of their productive weakness and of the loss of their old position as centres through which the country received its imports from abroad. Townsfolk and factory workers lack food, fuel, raw materials and much else that in a civilized State is considered a necessary of life. Thus, ten million poods of fish were caught last year, but there were no means of bringing them from the fisheries to the great industrial centres where they were most needed. Townsfolk are starving, and in winter, cold. People living in rooms in a flat, complete strangers to each other, by general agreement bring all their beds into the kitchen. In the kitchen soup is made once a day. There is a little warmth there beside the natural warmth of several human beings in a small room. There it is possible to sleep. During the whole of last winter, in the case I have in mind, there were no means of heating the other rooms, where the temperature was almost always far below freezing-point. It is difficult to make the conditions real except by individual examples. The lack of medicines, due directly to the blockade, seems to have small effect on the imagination when simply stated as such. Perhaps people will realize what it means when instead of talking of the wounded undergoing operations without anæsthetics I record the case of an acquaintance, a Bolshevik, working in a Government office, who suffered last summer from a slight derangement of the stomach due to improper and inadequate feeding.

29

His doctor prescribed a medicine, and nearly a dozen different apothecaries were unable to make up the prescription for lack of one or several of the simple ingredients required. Soap has become an article so rare (in Russia as in Germany during the blockade and the war there is a terrible absence of fats) that for the present it is to be treated as a means of safeguarding labor, to be given to the workmen for washing after and during their work, and in preference to miners, chemical, medical and sanitary workers, for whose efficiency and health it is essential. The proper washing of underclothes is impossible. To induce the population of Moscow to go to the baths during the typhus epidemic, it was a sufficient bribe to promise to each person beside the free bath a free scrap of soap. Houses are falling into disrepair for want of plaster, paint and tools. Nor is it possible to substitute one thing for another, for Russia's industries all suffer alike from their old dependence on the West, as well as from the inadequacy of the transport to bring to the factories the material they need. People remind each other that during the war the Germans, when similarly hard put to it for clothes, made paper dresses, table-cloths, etc. In Russia the nets used in paper-making are worn out. At last, in April, 1920 (so Lenin told me), there seemed to be a hope of getting new ones from abroad. But the condition of the paper industry is typical of all, in a country which, it should not be forgotten, could be in a position to supply wood-pulp for other countries besides itself. The factories are able to produce only sixty per cent. of demands that have previously, by the strictest scrutiny, been reduced to a minimum before they are made. The reasons, apart from the lack of nets and cloths, are summed up in absence of food, forage and finally labor. Even when wood is brought by river the trouble is not yet overcome. The horses are dead and eaten or starved and weak. Factories have to cease working so that the workmen, themselves under-fed, can drag the wood from the barges to the mills. It may well be imagined what the effect of hunger, cold, and the disheartenment consequent on such conditions of work and the seeming hopelessness of the position have on the productivity of labor, the fall in which reacts on all the industries, on transport, on the general situation and so again on itself.

Mr. J. M. Keynes, writing with Central Europe in his mind (he is, I think, as ignorant of Russia as I am of Germany), says: "What then is our picture of Europe? A country population able to support life on the fruits of its own agricultural production, but without the accustomed surplus for the towns, and also (as a result of the lack of imported materials, and so of variety and amount in the salable manufactures of the towns) without the usual incentives to market food in exchange for other wares; an industrial population unable to keep its strength for lack of food, unable to earn a livelihood for lack of materials, and so unable to make good by imports from abroad the failure of productivity at home."

Russia is an emphasized engraving, in which every line of that picture is bitten in with repeated washes of acid. Several new lines, however, are added to the drawing, for in Russia the processes at work elsewhere have gone further than in the rest of Europe, and it is possible to see dimly, in faint outline, the new stage of decay which is threatened. The struggle to arrest that decay is the real crisis of the revolution, of Russia, and, not impossibly, of Europe. For each country that develops to the end in this direction is a country lost to the economic comity of Europe. And, as one country follows another over the brink, so will the remaining countries be faced by conditions of increasingly narrow self-dependence, in fact by the very conditions which in Russia, so far, have received their clearest, most forcible illustration.

THE SHORTAGE OF MEN

In the preceding chapter I wrote of Russia's many wants, and of the processes visibly at work, tending to make her condition worse and not better. But I wrote of things, not of people. I wrote of the shortage of this and of that, but not of the most serious of all shortages, which, while itself largely due to those already discussed, daily intensifies them, and points the way to that further stage of decay which is threatened in the near future in Russia, and, in the more distant future, in Europe. I did not write of the shortage and deterioration of labor.

Shortage of labor is not peculiar to Russia. It is among the post-war phenomena common to all countries. The war and its accompanying diseases have cost Europe, including Russia, an enormous number of able-bodied men. Many millions of others have lost the habit of regular work.

34

German industrialists complain that they cannot get labor, and that when they get it, it is not productive. I heard complaints on the same subject in England. But just as the economic crisis, due in the first instance to the war and the isolation it imposed, has gone further in Russia than elsewhere, so the shortage of labor, at present a handicap, an annoyance in more fortunate countries, is in Russia perhaps the greatest of the national dangers. Shortage of labor cannot be measured simply by the decreasing numbers of the workmen. If it takes two workmen as long to do a particular job in 1920 as it took one man to do it in 1914, then, even if the number of workmen has remained the same, the actual supply of labor has been halved. And in Russia the situation is worse than that. For example, in the group of State metal-working factories, those, in fact which may be considered as the weapon with which Russia is trying to cut her way out of her transport difficulties, apart from the fact that there were in 1916 81,600 workmen, whereas in 1920 there are only 42,500, labor has deteriorated in the most appalling manner. In 1916 in these factories 92 per cent. of the nominal working hours were actually kept; in 1920 work goes on during only 60 per cent. of the nominal hours. It is estimated that the labor of a single workman produces now only one quarter of what it produced in 1916. To take another example, also from workmen engaged in transport, that is to say, in the most important of all work at the present time: in the Moscow junction of the Moscow Kazan Railway, between November 1st and February 29th (1920), 292 workmen and clerks missed 12,048 working days, being absent, on an average, forty days per man in the four months. In Moscow passenger-station on this line, 22 workmen missed in November 106 days, in December 273, in January 338, and in February 380; in an appalling crescendo further illustrated by the wagon department, where 28 workmen missed in November 104 days and in February 500. In November workmen absented themselves for single days. In February the same workmen were absent for the greater part of the month. The invariable excuse was illness. Many cases of illness there undoubtedly were, since this period was the worst of the typhus epidemic, but besides illness, and besides mere obvious idleness, which no doubt accounts for a certain proportion of illegitimate holidays, there is another explanation which goes nearer the root of the matter. Much of the time filched from the State was in all probability spent in expeditions in search of food. In Petrograd, the Council of Public Economy complain that there is a tendency to turn the eight-hour day into a four-hour day. Attempts are being made to arrest this tendency by making an additional food allowance conditional on the actual fulfilment of working days. In the Donetz coal basin, the monthly output per man was in 1914 750 poods, in 1916 615 poods, in 1919 240 poods (figures taken from Ekaterinoslav Government), and in 1920 the output per man is estimated at being something near 220 poods. In the shale mines on the Volga, where food conditions are comparatively good, productivity is comparatively high. Thus in a small mine near Simbirsk there are 230 workmen, of whom 50 to 60 are skilled. The output for the unskilled is 28.9 poods in a shift, for the skilled 68.3. But even there 25 per cent. of the workmen are regular absentees, and actually the mine works only 17 or 18 days in a month, that is, 70 per cent. of the normal number of working days. The remaining 30 per cent. of nominal working time is spent by the workmen in getting food. Another small mine in the same district is worked entirely by unskilled labor, the workers being peasants from the neighboring villages. In this mine the productivity per man is less, but all the men work full time. They do not have to waste time in securing food, because, being local peasants, they are supplied by their own villages and families. In Moscow and Petrograd food is far more difficult to secure, more time is wasted on that hopeless task; even with that waste of time, the workman is not properly fed, and it cannot be wondered at that his productivity is low.

Something, no doubt, is due to the natural character of the Russians, which led Trotsky to define man as an animal distinguished by laziness. Russians are certainly lazy, and probably owe to their climate their remarkable incapacity for prolonged effort. The Russian climate is such that over large areas of Russia the Russian peasant is accustomed, and has been accustomed for hundreds of years, to perform prodigies of labor during two short periods of sowing and harvest, and to spend the immensely long and monotonous winter in a hibernation like that of the snake or the dormouse. There is a much greater difference between a Russian workman's normal output and that of which he is capable for a short time if he sets himself to it, than there is between the normal and exceptional output of an Englishman, whose temperate climate has not taught him to regard a great part of the year as a period of mere waiting for and resting from the extraordinary effort of a few weeks.[1]

But this uneven working temperament was characteristic of the Russian before the war as well as now. It has been said that the revolution removed the stimulus to labor, and left the

[1] Given any particular motive, any particular enthusiasm, or visible, desirable object, even the hungry Russian workmen of to-day are capable of sudden and temporary increase of output. The "Saturdayings" (see p. 119) provide endless illustrations of this. They had something in the character of a picnic, they were novel, they were out of the routine, and the productivity of labor during a "Saturdaying" was invariably higher than on a weekday. For example, there is a shortage of paper for cigarettes. People roll cigarettes in old newspapers. It occurred to the Central Committee of the Papermakers' Union to organize a "Sundaying" with the object of sending cigarette paper to the soldiers in the Red Army. Six factories took part. Here is a table showing the output of

39

Russian laziness to have its way. In the first period of the revolution that may have been true. It is becoming day by day less true. The fundamental reasons of low productivity will not be found in any sudden or unusual efflorescence, of idleness, but in economic conditions which cannot but reduce the productivity of idle and industrious alike. Insufficient feeding is one such reason. The proportion of working time consumed in foraging is another. But the whole of my first chapter may be taken as a compact mass of reasons why the Russians at the present time should not work with anything like a normal productivity. It is said that bad workmen complain of their tools, but even good ones become disheartened if compelled to work with makeshifts, mended tools, on a stock of materials that runs

these factories during the "Sundaying" and the average weekday output. The figures are in poods.

Factory	Made on the Sunday	Average Weekday Output
Krasnogorodskaya	615	450
Griaznovskaya	65	45
Medianskaya	105	90
Dobruzhskaya	286	250
Belgiiskaya	127	85
Ropshinskaya	85	55

out from one day to the next, in factories where the machinery may come at any moment to a standstill from lack of fuel.

There would thus be a shortage of labor in Russia, even if the numbers of workmen were the same to-day as they were before the war. Unfortunately that is not so. Turning from the question of low productivity per man to that of absolute shortage of men: the example given at the beginning of this chapter, showing that in the most important group of factories the number of workmen has fallen 50 per cent. is by no means exceptional. Walking through the passages of what used to be the Club of the Nobles, and is now the house of the Trades Unions during the recent Trades Union Congress in Moscow, I observed among a number of pictorial diagrams on the walls, one in particular illustrating the rise and fall of the working population of Moscow during a number of years. Each year was represented by the picture of a factory with a chimney which rose and fell with the population. From that diagram I took the figures for 1913, 1918 and 1919. These figures should be constantly borne in mind by any one who wishes to realize how catastrophic the shortage of labor in Russia actually is, and to judge how sweeping may be the changes in the social configuration of the country if that shortage continues to increase. Here are the figures:

Workmen in Moscow in 1913 159,344
Workmen in Moscow in 1918 157,282
Workmen in Moscow in 1919 105,210

That is to say, that one-third of the workmen of Moscow ceased to live there, or ceased to be workmen, in the course of a single year. A similar phenomenon is observable in each one of the big industrial districts.

What has become of those workmen?

A partial explanation is obvious. The main impulse of the revolution came from the town workers. Of these, the metal workers were the most decided, and those who most freely joined the Red Guard in the early and the Red Army in the later days of the revolution. Many, in those early days, when there was more enthusiasm than discipline, when there were hardly any experienced officers, and those without much authority, were slaughtered during the German advance of 1918. The first mobilizations, when conscription was introduced, were among the workers in the great industrial districts. The troops from Petrograd and Moscow, exclusively workmen's regiments, have suffered more than any other during the civil war, being the most dependable and being thrown, like the guards of old time, into the worst place at any serious crisis. Many thousands of them have died for the sake of the revolution which, were they living, they would be hard put to it to save. (The special shortage of skilled workers is also partially to be explained by the indiscriminate mobilizations of 1914–15, when great numbers of the most valuable engineers and other skilled workers were thrown into the front line, and it was not until their loss was already felt that the Tsar's Government in this matter came belatedly to its senses.)

But these explanations are only partial. The more general answer to the question, What has become of the workmen? lies in the very economic crisis which their absence accentuates. Russia is unlike England, where starvation of the towns would be practically starvation of the whole island. In Russia, if a man is hungry, he has only to walk far enough and he will come to a place where there is plenty to eat. Almost every Russian worker retains in some form or other connection with a village, where, if he returns, he will not be an entire stranger, but at worst a poor relation, and quite possibly an honored guest. It is not surprising that many thousands have "returned to the land" in this way. Further, if a workman retains his connection, both with a distant village and with a town, he can keep himself and his family fat and prosperous by ceasing to be a workman, and, instead, travelling on the buffers or the roof of a railway wagon, and bringing back with him sacks of flour and potatoes for sale in the town at fantastic prices. Thereby he is lost to productive labor, and his uncomfortable but adventurous life becomes directly harmful, tending to increase the strain on transport, since it is obviously more economical to transport a thousand sacks than to transport a thousand sacks with an idle workman attached to each sack. Further, his activities actually make it more difficult for the town population to get food. By keeping open for the village the possibility of selling at fantastic prices, he lessens the readiness of the peasants to part with their flour at the lower prices of the Government. Nor is it as if his activities benefited the working population. The food he brings in goes for the most part to those who have plenty of money or have things to exchange for it. And honest men in Russia to-day have not much money, and those who have things to exchange are not as a rule workmen. The theory of this man's harmfulness is, I know, open to argument, but the practice at least is exactly as I have stated it, and is obviously attractive to the individual who prefers adventure on a full stomach to useful work on an empty. Setting aside the theory with its latent quarrel between Free Trade and State control, we can still recognize that each workman engaged in these pursuits has become an unproductive middleman, one of that very parasitic species which the revolutionaries had hoped to make unnecessary. It is bad from the revolutionary point of view if a workman is so employed, but it is no less bad from the point of view of people who do not care twopence about the revolution one way or the other, but do care about getting Russia on her feet again and out of her economic crisis. It is bad enough if an unskilled workman is so employed. It is far worse if a skilled workman finds he can do better for himself as a "food speculator" than by the exercise of his legitimate craft. From mines, from every kind of factory come complaints of the decreasing proportion of skilled to unskilled workmen. The superior intelligence of the skilled worker offers him definite advantages should he engage in these pursuits, and his actual skill gives him other advantages in the villages. He can leave his factory and go to the village, there on the spot to ply his trade or variations of it, when as a handy man, repairing tools, etc., he will make an easy living, and by lessening the dependence of the village on the town do as much as the "food speculator" in worsening the conditions of the workman he has left behind.

And with that we come to the general changes in the social geography of Russia which are threatened if the processes now at work continue unchecked. The relations between town and village are the fundamental problem of the revolution. Town and countryside are in sharp contradiction daily intensified by the inability of the towns to supply the country's needs. The town may be considered as a single productive organism, with feelers stretching into the country, and actual outposts there in the form of agricultural enterprises taking their directives from the centre and working as definite parts of the State organism. All round this town organism, in all its interstices, it too, with its feelers in the form of "food speculators," is the anarchic chaos of the country, consisting of a myriad independent units, regulated by no plan, without a brain centre of any kind. Either the organized town will hold its own against and gradually dominate and systematize the country chaos, or that chaos little by little will engulf the town organism. Every workman who leaves the town automatically places himself on the side of the country in that struggle. And when a town like Moscow loses a third of its working population in a year, it is impossible not to see that, so far, the struggle is going in favor of that huge chaotic, unconscious but immensely powerful countryside. There is even a danger that the town may become divided against itself. Just as scarcity of food leads to food speculation, so the shortage of labor is making

47

possible a sort of speculation in labor. The urgent need of labor has led to a resurrection of the methods of the direct recruiting of workmen in the villages by the agents of particular factories, who by exceptional terms succeed in getting workmen where the Government organs fail. And, of course, this recruiting is not confined to the villages. Those enterprises which are situated in the corn districts are naturally able to offer better conditions, for the sake of which workmen are ready to leave their jobs and skilled workmen to do unskilled work, and the result can only be a drainage of good workmen away from the hungry central industrial districts where they are most of all needed.

Summing up the facts collected in this chapter and in the first on the lack of things and the lack of men, I think the economic crisis in Russia may be fairly stated as follows: Owing to the appalling condition of Russian transport, and owing to the fact that since 1914 Russia has been practically in a state of blockade, the towns have lost their power of supplying, either as middlemen or as producers, the simplest needs of the villages. Partly owing to this, partly again because of the condition of transport, the towns are not receiving the necessaries of life in sufficient quantities. The result of this is a serious fall in the productivity of labor, and a steady flow of skilled and unskilled workmen from the towns towards the villages, and from employments the exercise of which tends to assist the towns in recovering their old position as essential sources of supply to employments that tend to have the opposite effect. If this continues unchecked, it will make impossible the regeneration of Russian industry, and will result in the increasing independence of the villages, which will tend to become entirely self-supporting communities, tilling the ground in a less and less efficient manner, with ruder tools, with less and less incentive to produce more than is wanted for the needs of the village itself. Russia, in these circumstances, may sink into something very like barbarism, for with the decay of the economic importance of the towns would decay also their authority, and free-booting on a small and large scale would become profitable and not very dangerous. It would be possible, no doubt, for foreigners to trade with the Russians as with the natives of the cannibal islands, bartering looking-glasses and cheap tools, but, should such a state of things come to be, it would mean long years of colonization, with all the new possibilities and risks involved in the subjugation of a free people, before Western Europe could count once more on getting a considerable portion of its food from Russian corn lands.

That is the position, those the natural tendencies at work. But opposed to these tendencies are the united efforts of the Communists and of those who, leaving the question of Communism discreetly aside, work with them for the sake of preventing such collapse of Russian civilization. They recognize the existence of every one of the tendencies I have described, but they are convinced that every one of these tendencies will be arrested. They believe that the country will not conquer the town but the reverse. So far from expecting the unproductive stagnation described in the last paragraph, they think of Russia as of the natural food supply of Europe, which the Communists among them believe will, in course of time, be made up for "Working Men's Republics" (though, for the sake of their own Republic, they are not inclined to postpone trade with Europe until that epoch arrives). At the very time when spades and sickles are wearing out or worn out, these men are determined that the food output of Russia shall sooner or later be increased by the introduction of better methods of agriculture and farming on a larger scale. We are witnessing in Russia the first stages of a titanic struggle, with on one side all the forces of nature leading apparently to an inevitable collapse of civilization, and on the other side nothing but the incalculable force of human will.

THE COMMUNIST DICTATORSHIP

How is that will expressed? What is the organization welded by adversity which, in this crisis, supersedes even the Soviet Constitution, and stands between this people and chaos?

It is a commonplace to say that Russia is ruled, driven if you like, cold, starving as she is, to effort after effort by the dictatorship of a party. It is a commonplace alike in the mouths of those who wish to make the continued existence of that organization impossible and in the mouths of the Communists themselves. At the second congress of the Third International, Trotsky remarked, "A party as such, in the course of the development of a revolution, becomes identical with the revolution." Lenin, on the same occasion, replying to a critic who said that he differed from the Communists in his understanding of what was meant by the Dictatorship of the Proletariat, said, "He says that we understand by the words 'Dictatorship of the Proletariat' what is actually the dictatorship of its determined and conscious minority. And that is the fact." Later he asked, "What is this minority? It may be called a party. If this minority is actually conscious, *if it is able to draw the masses after it*, if it shows itself capable of replying to every question on the agenda list of the political day, it actually constitutes a party." And Trotsky again, on the same occasion, illustrated the relative positions of the Soviet Constitution and the Communist Party when he said, "And to-day, now that we have received an offer of peace from the Polish Government, who decides the question? Whither are the workers to turn? We have our Council of People's Commissaries, of course, but that, too, must be under a certain control. Whose control? The control of the working class as a formless chaotic mass? No. The Central Committee of the party is called together to discuss and decide the question. And when we have to wage war, to form new divisions, to find the best elements for them—to whom do we turn? To the party, to the Central Committee. And it gives directives to the local committees, 'Send Communists to the front.' The case is precisely the same with the Agrarian question, with that of supply, and with all other questions whatsoever."

No one denies these facts, but their mere statement is quite inadequate to explain what is being done in Russia and how it is being done. I do not think it would be a waste of time to set down as briefly as possible, without the comments of praise or blame that would be inevitable from one primarily interested in the problem from the Capitalist or Communist point of view what, from observation and inquiry, I believe to be the main framework of the organization whereby that dictatorship of the party works.

The Soviet Constitution is not so much moribund as in abeyance. The Executive Committee, for example, which used to meet once a week or even oftener, now meets on the rarest occasions. Criticism on this account was met with the reply that the members of the Executive Committee were busy on the front and in various parts of Russia. As a matter of fact, the work which that Committee used to do is now done by the Central Committee of the Bolshevik Party, so that the bulk of the 150 members of the Central Executive are actually free for other work, a saving of something like 130 men. This does not involve any very great change, but merely an economy in the use of men. In the old days, as I well remember, the opening of a session of the Executive Committee was invariably late, the reason being that the various parties composing it had not yet finished their preliminary and private discussions. There is now an overwhelming Communist majority in the Executive Committee, as elsewhere. I think it may be regarded as proved that these majorities are not always legitimately obtained. Non-Communist delegates do undoubtedly find every kind of difficulty put in their way by the rather Jesuitical adherents of the faith. But, no matter how these majorities are obtained, the result is that when the Communist Party has made up its mind on any subject, it is so certain of being able to carry its point that the calling together of the All-Russian Executive Committee is merely a theatrical demonstration of the fact that it can do what it likes. When it does meet, the Communists allow the microscopical opposition great liberty of speech, listen quietly, cheer ironically, and vote like one man, proving on every occasion that the meeting of the Executive Committee was the idlest of forms, intended rather to satisfy purists than for purposes of discussion, since the real discussion has all taken place beforehand among the Communists themselves. Something like this must happen with every representative assembly at which a single party has a great preponderance and a rigid internal discipline. The real interest is in the discussion inside the Party Committees.

This state of affairs would probably be more actively resented if the people were capable of resenting anything but their own hunger, or of fearing anything but a general collapse which would turn that hunger into starvation. It must be remembered that the urgency of the economic crisis has driven political questions into the background. The Communists (compare Rykov's remarks on this subject, p. 175) believe that this is the natural result of social revolution. They think that political parties will disappear altogether and that people will band together, not for the victory of one of several contending political parties, but solely for economic coöperation or joint enterprise in art or science. In support of this they point to the number of their opponents who have become Communists, and to the still greater number of non-Communists who are loyally working with them for the economic reconstruction of the country. I do not agree with the Communists in this, nor yet with their opponents, who attribute the death of political discussion to fear of the Extraordinary Commission. I think that both the Communists and their opponents underestimate the influence of the economic ruin that affects everybody. The latter particularly, feeling that in some way they must justify themselves to politically minded foreign visitors, seek an excuse for their apathy in the one institution that is almost universally unpopular. I have many non-Communist friends in Russia, but have never detected the least restraint that could be attributed to fear of anybody in their criticisms of the Communist régime. The fear existed alike among Communists and non-Communists, but it was like the fear of people walking about in a particularly bad thunderstorm. The activities and arrests of the Extraordinary Commission are so haphazard, often so utterly illogical, that it is quite idle for any one to say to himself that by following any given line of conduct he will avoid molestation. Also, there is something in the Russian character which makes any prohibition of discussion almost an invitation to discuss. I have never met a Russian who could be prevented from saying whatever he liked whenever he liked, by any threats or dangers whatsoever. The only way to prevent a Russian from talking is to cut out his tongue. The real reason for the apathy is that, for the moment, for almost everybody, political questions are of infinitesimal importance in comparison with questions of food and warmth. The ferment of political discussion that filled the first years of the revolution has died away, and people talk about little but what they are able to get for dinner, or what somebody else has been able to get. I, like other foreign visitors coming to Russia after feeding up in other countries, am all agog to make people talk. But the sort of questions which interest me, with my full-fed stomach, are brushed aside almost fretfully by men who have been more or less hungry for two or three years on end.

I find, instead of an urgent desire to alter this

or that at once, to-morrow, in the political complexion of the country, a general desire to do the best that can be done with things as they are, a general fear of further upheaval of any kind, in fact a general acquiescence in the present state of affairs politically, in the hope of altering the present state of affairs economically. And this is entirely natural. Everybody, Communists included, rails bitterly at the inefficiencies of the present system, but everybody, Anti-Communists included, admits that there is nothing whatever capable of taking its place. Its failure is highly undesirable, not because it itself is good, but because such failure would be preceded or followed by a breakdown of all existing organizations. Food distribution, inadequate as it now is, would come to an end. The innumerable non-political committees, which are rather like Boards of Directors controlling the Timber, Fur, Fishery, Steel, Matches or other Trusts (since the nationalized industries can be so considered) would collapse, and with them would collapse not only yet one more hope of keeping a breath of life in Russian industry, but also the actual livelihoods of a great number of people, both Communists and non-

Communists. I do not think it is realized outside Russia how large a proportion of the educated classes have become civil servants of one kind or another. It is a rare thing when a whole family has left Russia, and many of the most embittered partisans of war on Russia have relations inside Russia who have long ago found places under the new system, and consequently fear its collapse as much as any one. One case occurs to me in which a father was an important minister in one of the various White Governments which have received Allied support, while his son inside Russia was doing pretty well as a responsible official under the Communists. Now in the event of a violent change, the Communists would be outlaws with a price on every head, and those who have worked with them, being Russians, know their fellow-countrymen well enough to be pretty well convinced that the mere fact that they are without cards of the membership of the Communist Party, would not save them in the orgy of slaughter that would follow any such collapse.

People may think that I underestimate the importance of the Extraordinary Commission. I am perfectly aware that without this police force with its spies, its prisons and its troops, the difficulties of the Dictatorship would be increased by every kind of disorder, and the chaos, which I still fear may come, would have begun long ago. I believe, too, that the overgrown power of the Extraordinary Commission, and the cure that must sooner or later be applied to it, may, as in the French Revolution, bring about the collapse of the whole system. The Commission depends for its strength on the fear of something else. I have seen it weaken when there was a hope of general peace. I have seen it tighten its grip in the presence of attacks from without and attempted assassination within. It is dreaded by everybody; not even Communists are safe from it; but it does not suffice to explain the Dictatorship, and is actually entirely irrelevant to the most important process of that Dictatorship, namely, the adoption of a single idea, a single argument, by the whole of a very large body of men. The whole power of the Extraordinary Commission does not affect in the slightest degree discussions inside the Communist Party, and those discussions are the simple fact distinguishing the Communist

Dictatorship from any of the other dictatorships by which it may be supplanted.

There are 600,000 members of the Communist Party (611,978 on April 2, 1920). There are nineteen members of the Central Committee of that party. There are, I believe, five who, when they agree, can usually sway the remaining fourteen. There is no need to wonder how these fourteen can be argued into acceptance of the views of the still smaller inner ring, but the process of persuading the six hundred thousand of the desirability of, for example, such measures as those involved in industrial conscription which, at first sight, was certainly repugnant to most of them, is the main secret of the Dictatorship, and is not in any way affected by the existence of the Extraordinary Commission.

Thus the actual government of Russia at the present time may be not unfairly considered as a small group inside the Central Committee of the Communist Party. This small group is able to persuade the majority of the remaining members of that Committee. The Committee then sets about persuading the majority of the party. In the case of important measures the process is elaborate. The Committee issues a statement of its case, and the party newspapers the *Pravda* and its affiliated organs are deluged with its discussion. When this discussion has had time to spread through the country, congresses of Communists meet in the provincial centres, and members of the Central Committee go down to these conferences to defend the "theses" which the Committee has issued. These provincial congresses, exclusively Communist, send their delegates of an All-Russian Congress. There the "theses" of the Central Committee get altered, confirmed, or, in the case of an obviously unpersuaded and large opposition in the party, are referred back or in other ways shelved. Then the delegates, even those who have been in opposition at the congress, go back to the country pledged to defend the position of the majority. This sometimes has curious results. For example, I heard Communist Trades Unionists fiercely arguing against certain clauses in the theses on industrial conscription at a Communist Congress at the Kremlin; less than a week afterwards I heard these same men defending precisely these clauses at a Trades Union Congress over the way, they loyally abiding by the collective opinion of their fellow Communists and subject to particularly uncomfortable heckling from people who vociferously reminded them (since the Communist debates had been published) that they were now defending what, a few days before, they had vehemently attacked.

The great strength of the Communist Party is comparable to the strength of the Jesuits, who, similarly, put themselves and their opinions at the disposal of the body politic of their fellow members. Until a decision had been made, a Communist is perfectly free to do his best to prevent it being made, to urge alterations in it, or to supply a rival decision, but once it has been made he will support it without changing his private opinion. In all mixed congresses, rather than break the party discipline, he will give his vote for it, speak in favor of it, and use against its adversaries the very arguments that have been used against himself. He has his share in electing the local Communist Committee, and, indirectly, in electing the all-powerful Central Committee of the party, and he binds himself to do at any moment in his life exactly what these

Committees decide for him. These Committees decide the use that is to be made of the lives, not only of the rank and file of the party, but also of their own members. Even a member of the Central Committee does not escape. He may be voted by his fellow members into leaving a job he likes and taking up another he detests in which they think his particular talents will better serve the party aims. To become a member of the Communist Party involves a kind of intellectual abdication, or, to put it differently, a readiness at any moment to place the collective wisdom of the party's Committee above one's individual instincts or ideas. You may influence its decisions, you may even get it to endorse your own, but Lenin himself, if he were to fail on any occasion to obtain the agreement of a majority in the Central Committee, would have to do precisely what the Committee should tell him. Lenin's opinion carries great weight because he is Lenin, but it carries less weight than that of the Central Committee, of which he forms a nineteenth part. On the other hand, the opinion of Lenin and a very small group of outstanding figures is supported by great prestige inside the

Committee, and that of the Committee is supported by overwhelming prestige among the rank and file. The result is that this small group is nearly always sure of being able to use the whole vote of 600,000 Communists in the realization of its decisions.

Now 600,000 men and women acting on the instructions of a highly centralized directive, all the important decisions of which have been thrashed out and re-thrashed until they have general support within the party; 600,000 men and women prepared, not only to vote in support of these decisions, but with a carefully fostered readiness to sacrifice their lives for them if necessary; 600,000 men and women who are persuaded that by their way alone is humanity to be saved; who are persuaded (to put it as cynically and unsympathetically as possible) that the noblest death one can die is in carrying out a decision of the Central Committee; such a body, even in a country such as Russia, is an enormously strong embodiment of human will, an instrument of struggle capable of working something very like miracles. It can be and is controlled like an army in battle. It can mobilize its members, 10 per cent. of them, 50 per cent., the local Committees choosing them, and send them to the front when the front is in danger, or to the railways and repair shops when it is decided that the weakest point is that of transport. If its only task were to fight those organizations of loosely knit and only momentarily united interests which are opposed to it, those jerry-built alliances of Reactionaries with Liberals, United-Indivisible-Russians with Ukrainians, Agrarians with Sugar-Refiners, Monarchists with Republicans, that task would long ago have been finished. But it has to fight something infinitely stronger than these in fighting the economic ruin of Russia, which, if it is too strong, too powerful to be arrested by the Communists, would make short work of those who are without any such fanatic single-minded and perfectly disciplined organization.

A CONFERENCE AT JAROSLAVL

I HAVE already suggested that although the small
Central Committee of the Communist Party does
invariably get its own way, there are essential
differences between this Dictatorship and the dictatorship of, for example, a General. The main
difference is that whereas the General merely
writes an order about which most people hear for
the first time only when it is promulgated, the
Central Committee prepares the way for its dicta-
tion by a most elaborate series of discussions and
counter discussions throughout the country,
whereby it wins the bulk of the Communist Party
to its opinion, after which it proceeds through
local and general congresses to do the same with
the Trades Unions. This done, a further series
of propaganda meetings among the people actually to be affected smooths the way for the
introduction of whatever new measure is being

68

carried through at the moment. All this talk, besides lessening the amount of physical force necessary in carrying out a decision, must also avoid, at least in part, the deadening effect that would be caused by mere compulsory obedience to the unexplained orders of a military dictator. Of the reality of the Communist Dictatorship I have no sort of doubt. But its methods are such as tend towards the awakening of a political consciousness which, if and when normal conditions—of feeding and peace, for example—are attained, will make dictatorship of any kind almost impossible.

To illustrate these methods of the Dictatorship, I cannot do better than copy into this book some pages of my diary written in March of this year when I was present at one of the provincial conferences which were held in preparation of the All-Russian Communist Conference at the end of the month.

At seven in the evening Radek called for me and took me to the Jaroslavl station, where we met Larin, whom I had known in 1918. An old Menshevik, he was the originator and most urgent supporter of the decree annulling the foreign debts. He is a very ill man, partially paralyzed, having to use both hands even to get food to his mouth or to turn over the leaves of a book. In spite of this he is one of the hardest workers in Russia, and although his obstinacy, his hatred of compromise, and a sort of mixed originality and perverseness keep him almost permanently at loggerheads with the Central Committee, he retains everybody's respect because of the real heroism with which he conquers physical disabilities which long ago would have overwhelmed a less unbreakable spirit. Both Radek and Larin were going to the Communist Conference at Jaroslavl which was to consider the new theses of the Central Committee of the party with regard to Industrial Conscription. Radek was going to defend the position of the Central Committee, Larin to defend his own. Both are old friends. As Radek said to me, he intended to destroy Larin's position, but not, if he could help it, prevent Larin being nominated among the Jaroslavl delegates to All-Russian Conference which was in preparation. Larin, whose work keeps him continually traveling, has his own car, specially arranged so that his uninterrupted labor shall have as little effect as possible on his dangerously frail body. Radek and I traveled in one of the special cars of the Central Executive Committee, of which he is a member.

The car seemed very clean, but, as an additional precaution, we began by rubbing turpentine on our necks and wrists and angles for the discouragement of lice, now generally known as "Semashki" from the name of Semashko, the Commissar of Public Health, who wages unceasing war for their destruction as the carriers of typhus germs. I rubbed the turpentine so energetically into my neck that it burnt like a collar of fire, and for a long time I was unable to get to sleep.

In the morning Radek, the two conductors who had charge of the wagons and I sat down together to breakfast and had a very merry meal, they providing cheese and bread and I a tin of corned beef providently sent out from home by the *Manchester Guardian*. We cooked up some coffee on a little spirit stove, which, in a neat basket together with plates, knives, forks, etc. (now almost unobtainable in Russia) had been a parting present from the German Spartacists to Radek when he was released from prison in Berlin and allowed to leave Germany.

The morning was bright and clear, and we had an excellent view of Jaroslavl when we drove from the station to the town, which is a mile or so off the line of the railway. The sun poured down on the white snow, on the barges still frozen into the Volga River, and on the gilt and painted domes and cupolas of the town. Many of the buildings had been destroyed during the rising artificially provoked in July, 1918, and its subsequent suppression. More damage was done then than was necessary, because the town was recaptured by troops which had been deserted by most of their officers, and therefore hammered away with artillery without any very definite plan of attack. The more important of the damaged buildings, such as the waterworks and the power station, have been repaired, the tramway was working, and, after Moscow, the town seemed clean, but plenty of ruins remained as memorials of that wanton and unjustifiable piece of folly which, it was supposed, would be the signal for a general rising.

We drove to the Hotel Bristol, now the headquarters of the Jaroslavl Executive Committee, where Rostopchin, the president, discussed with Larin and Radek the programme arranged for the conference. It was then proposed that we should have something to eat, when a very curious state of affairs (and one extremely Russian) was revealed. Rostopchin admitted that the commissariat arrangements of the Soviet and its Executive Committee were very bad. But in the center of the town there is a nunnery which was very badly damaged during the bombardment and is now used as a sort of prison or concentration camp for a Labor Regiment. Peasants from the surrounding country who have refused to give up their proper contribution of corn, or have otherwise disobeyed the laws, are, for punishment, lodged here, and made to expiate their sins by work. It so happens, Rostopchin explained, that the officer in charge of the prison feeding arrangements is a very energetic fellow, who had served in the old army in a similar capacity, and the meals served out to the prisoners are so much better than those produced in the Soviet headquarters, that the members of the Executive Committee

73

make a practice of walking over to the prison to dine. They invited us to do the same. Larin did not feel up to the walk, so he remained in the Soviet House to eat an inferior meal, while Radek and I, with Rostopchin and three other members of the local committee walked round to the prison. The bell tower of the old nunnery had been half shot away by artillery, and is in such a precarious condition that it is proposed to pull it down. But on passing under it we came into a wide courtyard surrounded by two-story whitewashed buildings that seemed scarcely to have suffered at all. We found the refectory in one of these buildings. It was astonishingly clean. There were wooden tables, of course without cloths, and each man had a wooden spoon and a hunk of bread. A great bowl of really excellent soup was put down in the middle of table, and we fell to hungrily enough. I made more mess on the table than any one else, because it requires considerable practice to convey almost boiling soup from a distant bowl to one's mouth without spilling it in a shallow wooden spoon four inches in diameter, and, having got it to one's mouth, to get any of it in without slopping over on either side. The regular diners there seemed to find no difficulty in it at all. One of the prisoners who mopped up after my disasters said I had better join them for a week, when I should find it quite easy. The soup bowl was followed by a fry of potatoes, quantities of which are grown in the district. For dealing with these I found the wooden spoon quite efficient. After that we had glasses of some sort of substitute for tea.

The Conference was held in the town theatre. There was a hint of comedy in the fact that the orchestra was playing the prelude to some very cheerful opera before the curtain rang up. Radek characteristically remarked that such music should be followed by something more sensational than a conference, proposed to me that we should form a tableau to illustrate the new peaceful policy of England with regard to Russia. As it was a party conference, I had really no right to be there, but Radek had arranged with Rostopchin that I should come in with himself, and be allowed to sit in the wings at the side of the stage. On the stage were Rostopchin, Radek, Larin and various members of the Communist Party Committee in the district.   Everything was ready, but the orchestra went on with its jig music on the other side of the curtain.   A message was sent to them. The music stopped with a jerk.   The curtain rose, disclosing a crowded auditorium.   Everybody stood up, both on the stage and in the theater, and sang, accompanied by the orchestra, first the "Internationale" and then the song for those who had died for the revolution.   Then, except for two or three politically minded musicians, the orchestra vanished away and the Conference began.

Unlike many of the meetings and conferences at which I have been present in Russia, this Jaroslavl Conference seemed to me to include practically none but men and women who either were or had been actual manual workers.   I looked over row after row of faces in the theatre, and could only find two faces which I thought might be Jewish, and none that obviously belonged to the "intelligentsia."   I found on inquiry that only three of the Communists present, excluding Radek and Larin, were old exiled and imprisoned revolutionaries of the educated class. Of these, two were on the platform.   All the rest were from the working class. The great majority of them, of course, had joined the Communists in 1917, but a dozen or so had been in the party as long ago as the first Russian revolution of 1905.

Radek, who was tremendously cheered (his long imprisonment in Germany, during which time few in Russia thought that they would see him alive again, has made him something of a popular hero) made a long, interesting and pugnacious speech setting out the grounds on which the Central Committee base their ideas about Industrial Conscription. These ideas are embodied in the series of theses issued by the Central Committee in January (see p. 134). Larin, who was very tired after the journey and patently conscious that Radek was a formidable opponent, made a speech setting out his reasons for differing with the Central Committee, and proposed an ingenious resolution, which, while expressing approval of the general position of the Committee, included four supplementary modifications which, as a matter of fact, nullified that position altogether. It was then about ten at night, and the Conference adjourned. We drove round to the prison in sledges, and by way of supper had some more soup and potatoes, and so back to the railway station to sleep in the cars.

Next day the Conference opened about noon, when there was a long discussion of the points at issue. Workman after workman came to the platform and gave his view. Some of the speeches were a little naïve, as when one soldier said that Comrades Lenin and Trotsky had often before pointed out difficult roads, and that whenever they had been followed they had shown the way to victory, and that therefore, though there was much in the Central Committee's theses that was hard to digest, he was for giving them complete support, confident that, as Comrades Lenin and Trotsky were in favor of them, they were likely to be right this time, as so often heretofore. But for the most part the speeches were directly concerned with the problem under discussion, and showed a political consciousness which would have been almost incredible three years ago. The Red Army served as a text for many, who said that the methods which had produced that army and its victories over the Whites had been proved successful and should be used to produce a Red Army of Labor and similar victories on the bloodless front against economic disaster. Nobody seemed to question the main idea of compulsory labor. The contest that aroused real bitterness was between the methods of individual and collegiate command. The new proposals lead eventually towards individual command, and fears were expressed lest this should mean putting summary powers into the hands of bourgeois specialists, thus nullifying "workers' control." In reply, it was pointed out that individual command had proved necessary in the army and had resulted in victory for the revolution. The question was not between specialists and no specialists. Everybody knew that specialists were necessary. The question was how to get the most out of them. Effective political control had secured that bourgeois specialists, old officers, led to victory the army of the Red Republic. The same result could be secured in the factories in the same way. It was pointed out that in one year they had succeeded in training 32,000 Red Commanders, that is to say, officers from the working class itself, and that it was not Utopian to hope and work for a similar output of workmen specialists, technically trained, and therefore themselves qualified for individual command in the factories. Meawhile there was nothing against the employment of Political Commissars in the factories as formerly in the regiments, to control in other than technical matters the doings of the specialists. On the other hand, it was said that the appointment of Commissars would tend to make Communists unpopular, since inevitably in many cases they would have to support the specialists against the workmen, and that the collegiate system made the workmen feel that they were actually the masters, and so gave possibilities of enthusiastic work not otherwise obtainable. This last point was hotly challenged. It was said that collegiate control meant little in effect, except waste of time and efficiency, because at worst work was delayed by disputes and at best the workmen members of the college merely countersigned the orders decided upon by the specialists. The enthusiastic work was said to be a fairy story. If it were really to be found then there would be no need for a conference to discover how to get it.

The most serious opposition, or at least the

most serious argument put forward, for there was less opposition than actual discussion, came from some of the representatives of the Trade Unionists. A good deal was said about the position of the Trades Unions in a Socialist State. There was general recognition that since the Trade Unions themselves controlled the conditions of labor and wages, the whole of their old work of organizing strikes against capitalists had ceased to have any meaning, since to strike now would be to strike against their own decisions. At the same time, certain tendencies to Syndicalism were still in existence, tendencies which might well lead to conflict between different unions, so that, for example, the match makers or the metal workers might wish to strike a bargain with the State, as of one country with another, and this might easily lead to a complete collapse of the socialist system.

The one thing on which the speakers were in complete agreement was the absolute need of an effort in industry equal to, if not greater than, the effort made in the army. I thought it significant that in many of the speeches the importance of this effort was urged as the only possible means of retaining the support of the peasants. There was a tacit recognition that the Conference represented town workers only. Larin, who had belonged to the old school which had grown up with its eyes on the industrial countries of the West and believed that revolution could be brought about by the town workers alone, that it was exclusively their affair, and that all else was of minor importance, unguardedly spoke of the peasant as "our neighbor." In Javoslavl, country and town are too near to allow the main problem of the revolution to be thus easily dismissed. It was instantly pointed out that the relation was much more intimate, and that, even if it were only "neighborly," peace could not long be preserved if it were continually necessary for one neighbor to steal the chickens of the other. These town workers of a district for the most part agricultural were very sure that the most urgent of all tasks was to raise industry to the point at which the town would really be able to supply the village with its needs.

Larin and Radek severally summed up and made final attacks on each other's positions, after which Radek's resolution approving the theses of the Central Committee was passed almost unanimously. Larin's four amendments received 1, 3, 7 and 1 vote apiece. This result was received with cheering throughout the theater, and showed the importance of such Conferences in smoothing the way of the Dictatorship, since it had been quite obvious when the discussion began that a very much larger proportion of the delegates than finally voted for his resolution had been more or less in sympathy with Larin in his opposition to the Central Committee.

There followed elections to the Party Conference in Moscow. Rostopchin, the president, read a list which had been submitted by the various *ouyezds* in the Jaroslavl Government. They were to send to Moscow fifteen delegates with the right to vote, together with another fifteen with the right to speak but not to vote. Larin, who had done much work in the district, was mentioned as one of the fifteen voting delegates, but he stood up and said that as the Conference had so clearly expressed its disagreement with his views, he thought it better to withdraw his candidature. Rostopchin put it to the Conference that although they disagreed with Larin, yet it

would be as well that he should have the opportunity of stating his views at the All-Russian
Conference, so that discussion there should be as
final and as many-sided as possible. The Conference expressed its agreement with this. Larin
withdrew his withdrawal, and was presently
elected. The main object of these conferences in
unifying opinion and in arming Communists with
argument for the defence of this unified opinion
among the masses was again illustrated when the
Conference, in leaving it to the *ouyezds* to choose
for themselves the non-voting delegates urged
them to select wherever possible people who
would have the widest opportunities of explaining on their return to the district whatever results might be reached in Moscow.

It was now pretty late in the evening, and
after another very satisfactory visit to the prison
we drove back to the station. Larin, who was
very disheartened, realizing that he had lost much
support in the course of the discussion, settled
down to work, and buried himself in a mass of
statistics. I prepared to go to bed, but we had
hardly got into the car when there was a tap at
the door and a couple of railwaymen came in.

They explained that a few hundred yards away along the line a concert and entertainment arranged by the Jaroslavl railwaymen was going on, and that their committee, hearing that Radek was at the station, had sent them to ask him to come over and say a few words to them if he were not too tired.

"Come along," said Radek, and we walked in the dark along the railway lines to a big one-story wooden shanty, where an electric lamp lit a great placard, "Railwaymen's Reading Room." We went into a packed hall. Every seat was occupied by railway workers and their wives and children. The gangways on either side were full of those who had not found room on the benches. We wriggled and pushed our way through this crowd, who were watching a play staged and acted by the railwaymen themselves, to a side door, through which we climbed up into the wings, and slid across the stage behind the scenery into a tiny dressing-room. Here Radek was laid hold of by the Master of the Ceremonies, who, it seemed, was also part editor of a railwaymen's newspaper, and made to give a long account of the present situation of Soviet Russia's Foreign

Affairs. The little box of a room filled to a solid mass as policemen, generals and ladies of the old régime threw off their costumes, and, in their working clothes, plain signal-men and engine-drivers, pressed round to listen. When the act ended, one of the railwaymen went to the front of the stage and announced that Radek, who had lately come back after imprisonment in Germany for the cause of revolution, was going to talk to them about the general state of affairs. I saw Radek grin at this forecast of his speech. I understood why, when he began to speak. He led off by a direct and furious onslaught on the railway workers in general, demanding work, work and more work, telling them that as the Red Army had been the vanguard of the revolution hitherto, and had starved and fought and given lives to save those at home from Denikin and Kolchak, so now it was the turn of the railway workers on whose efforts not only the Red Army but also the whole future of Russia depended. He addressed himself to the women, telling them in very bad Russian that unless their men worked superhumanly they would see their babies die from starvation next winter. I saw women nudge their husbands as they listened. Instead of giving them a pleasant, interesting sketch of the international position, which, no doubt, was what they had expected, he took the opportunity to tell them exactly how things stood at home. And the amazing thing was that they seemed to be pleased. They listened with extreme attention, wanted to turn out some one who had a sneezing fit at the far end of the hall, and nearly lifted the roof off with cheering when Radek had done. I wondered what sort of reception a man would have who in another country interrupted a play to hammer home truths about the need of work into an audience of working men who had gathered solely for the purpose of legitimate recreation. It was not as if he sugared the medicine he gave them. His speech was nothing but demands for discipline and work, coupled with prophecy of disaster in case work and discipline failed. It was delivered like all his speeches, with a strong Polish accent and a steady succession of mistakes in grammar.

As we walked home along the railway lines, half a dozen of the railwaymen pressed around Radek, and almost fought with each other as to who should walk next to him. And Radek, entirely happy, delighted at his success in giving them a bombshell instead of a bouquet, with one stout fellow on one arm, another on the other, two or three more listening in front and behind, continued rubbing it into them until we reached our wagon, when, after a general handshaking, they disappeared into the night.

THE TRADE UNIONS

TRADE Unions in Russia are in a different position from that which is common to all other Trades Unions in the world. In other countries the Trades Unions are a force with whose opposition the Government must reckon. In Russia the Government reckons not on the possible opposition of the Trades Unions, but on their help for realizing its most difficult measures, and for undermining and overwhelming any opposition which those measures may encounter. The Trades Unions in Russia, instead of being an organization outside the State protecting the interests of a class against the governing class, have become a part of the State organization. Since, during the present period of the revolution the backbone of the State organization is the Communist Party, the Trade Unions have come to be practically an extension of the party organization. This, of course, would be indignantly denied both by Trade Unionists and Communists. Still, in the preface to the All-Russian Trades Union Reports for 1919, Glebov, one of the best-known Trade Union leaders whom I remember in the spring of last year objecting to the use of bourgeois specialists in their proper places, admits as much in the following muddle-headed statement:—

"The base of the proletarian dictatorship is the Communist Party, which in general directs all the political and economic work of the State, leaning, first of all, on the Soviets as on the more revolutionary form of dictatorship of the proletariat, and secondly on the Trades Unions, as organizations which economically unite the proletariat of factory and workshop as the vanguard of the revolution, and as organizations of the new socialistic construction of the State. Thus the Trade Unions must be considered as a base of the Soviet State, as an organic form complementary to the other forms of the Proletariat Dictatorship." These two elaborate sentences constitute an admission of what I have just said.

Trades Unionists of other countries must regard the fate of their Russian colleagues with horror or with satisfaction, according to their views of events in Russia taken as a whole. If they do not believe that there has been a social revolution in Russia, they must regard the present position of the Russian Trades Unions as the reward of a complete defeat of Trade Unionism, in which a Capitalist government has been able to lay violent hands on the organization which was protecting the workers against it. If, on the other hand, they believe that there has been a social revolution, so that the class organized in Trades Unions is now identical with the governing class (of employers, etc.) against which the Unions once struggled, then they must regard the present position as a natural and satisfactory result of victory.

When I was in Moscow in the spring of this year, the Russian Trades Unions received a telegram from the Trades Union Congress at Amsterdam, a telegram which admirably illustrated the impossibility of separating judgment of the present position of the Unions from judgments of the Russian revolution as a whole. It encouraged the Unions "in their struggle" and promised support in that struggle. The Communists immediately asked "What struggle? Against the capitalist system in Russia which does not exist? Or against capitalist systems outside Russia?" They said that either the telegram meant this latter only, or it meant that its writers did not believe that there had been a social revolution in Russia. The point is arguable. If one believes that revolution is an impossibility, one can reason from that belief and say that in spite of certain upheavals in Russia the fundamental arrangement of society is the same there as in other countries, so that the position of the Trades Unions there must be the same, and, as in other countries they must be still engaged in augmenting the dinners of their members at the expense of the dinners of the capitalists which, in the long run (if that were possible) they would abolish. If, on the other hand, one believes that social revolution has actually occurred, to speak of Trades Unions continuing the struggle in which they conquered something like three years ago, is to urge them to a sterile fanaticism which has been neatly described by Professor Santayana as a redoubling of your effort when you have forgotten your aim.

It is probably true that the "aim" of the Trades Unions was more clearly defined in Russia than elsewhere. In England during the greater part of their history the Trades Unions have not been in conscious opposition to the State. In Russia this position was forced on the Trades Unions almost before they had had time to get to work. They were born, so to speak, with red flags in their hands. They grew up under circumstances of extreme difficulty and persecution. From 1905 on they were in decided opposition to the existing system, and were revolutionary rather than merely mitigatory organizations.

Before 1905 they were little more than associations for mutual help, very weak, spending most of their energies in self-preservation from the police, and hiding their character as class organizations by electing more or less Liberal managers and employers as "honorary members." 1905, however, settled their revolutionary character. In September of that year there was a Conference at Moscow, where it was decided to call an All-Russian Trades Union Congress. Reaction in Russia made this impossible, and the most they could do was to have another small

93

Conference in February, 1906, which, however, defined their object as that of creating a general Trade Union Movement organized on All-Russian lines. The temper of the Trades Unions then, and the condition of the country at that time, may be judged from the fact that although they were merely working for the right to form Unions, the right to strike, etc., they passed the following significant resolution: "Neither from the present Government *nor from the future State Duma* can be expected realization of freedom of coalition. . . . This Conference considers the legalization of the Trades Unions under present conditions absolutely impossible." The Conference was right. For twelve years after that there were no Trades Unions Conferences in Russia. Not until June, 1917, three months after the March Revolution, was the third Trade Union Conference able to meet. This Conference re-affirmed the revolutionary character of the Russian Trades Unions.

At that time the dominant party in the Soviets was that of the Mensheviks, who were opposed to the formation of a Soviet Government, and were supporting the provisional Cabinet of Kerensky.

The Trades Unions were actually at that time more revolutionary than the Soviets. This third Conference passed several resolutions, which show clearly enough that the present position of the Unions has not been brought about by any violence of the Communists from without, but was definitely promised by tendencies inside the Unions at a time when the Communists were probably the least authoritative party in Russia. This Conference of June, 1917, resolved that the Trades Unions should not only "remain militant class organizations . . . but . . . should support the activities of the Soviets of soldiers and workers' deputies." They thus clearly showed on which side they stood in the struggle then proceeding. Nor was this all. They also, though the Mensheviks were still the dominant party, resolved on that system of internal organizations and grouping, which has been actually realized under the Communists. I quote again from the resolution of this Conference:

"The evolution of the economic struggle demands from the workers such forms of professional organization as, basing themselves on the connection between various groups of workers in

95

the process of production, should unite within a general organization, and under general leadership, as large masses of workers as possible occupied in enterprises of the same kind, or in similar professions. With this object the workers should organize themselves professionally, not by shops or trades, but by productions, so that all the workers of a given enterprise should belong to one Union, even if they belong to different professions and even different productions." That which was then no more than a design is now an accurate description of Trades Union organization in Russia. Further, much that at present surprises the foreign inquirer was planned and considered desirable then, before the Communists had won a majority either in the Unions or in the Soviet. Thus this same third Conference resolved that "in the interests of greater efficiency and success in the economic struggle, a professional organization should be built on the principle of *democratic centralism*, assuring to every member a share in the affairs of the organization and, at the same time, obtaining unity in the leadership of the struggle." Finally, "Unity in the direction (leadership) of the economic struggle demands unity in the exchequer of the Trades Unions."

The point that I wish to make in thus illustrating the pre-Communist tendencies of the Russian Trades Unions is not simply that if their present position is undesirable they have only themselves to thank for it, but that in Russia the Trades Union movement before the October Revolution was working in the direction of such a revolution, that the events of October represented something like a Trade Union victory, so that the present position of the Unions as part of the organization defending that victory, as part of the system of government set up by that revolution, is logical and was to be expected. I have illustrated this from resolutions, because these give statements in words easily comparable with what has come to pass. It would be equally easy to point to deeds instead of words if we need more forcible though less accurate illustrations.

Thus, at the time of the Moscow Congress the Soviets, then Mensheviks, who were represented at the Congress (the object of the Congress was to whip up support for the Coalition Government) were against strikes of protest. The

Trades Unions took a point of view nearer that of the Bolsheviks, and the strikes in Moscow took place in spite of the Soviets. After the Kornilov affair, when the Mensheviks were still struggling for coalition with the bourgeois parties, the Trades Unions quite definitely took the Bolshevik standpoint. At the so-called Democratic Conference, intended as a sort of lifebelt for the sinking Provisional Government, only eight of the Trades Union delegates voted for a continuance of the coalition, whereas seventy-three voted against.

This consciously revolutionary character throughout their much shorter existence has distinguished Russian from, for example, English Trades Unions. It has set their course for them.

In October, 1917, they got the revolution for which they had been asking since March. Since then, one Congress after another has illustrated the natural and inevitable development of Trades Unions inside a revolutionary State which, like most if not all revolutionary States, is attacked simultaneously by hostile armies from without and by economic paralysis from within. The excited and lighthearted Trades Unionists of three years ago, who believed that the mere decreeing of "workers' control" would bring all difficulties automatically to an end, are now unrecognizable. We have seen illusion after illusion scraped from them by the pumice-stone of experience, while the appalling state of the industries which they now largely control, and the ruin of the country in which they attained that control, have forced them to alter their immediate aims to meet immediate dangers, and have accelerated the process of adaptation made inevitable by their victory.

The process of adaptation has had the natural result of producing new internal cleavages. Change after change in their programme and theory of the Russian Trades Unionists has been due to the pressure of life itself, to the urgency of struggling against the worsening of conditions already almost unbearable. It is perfectly natural that those Unions which hold back from adaptation and resent the changes are precisely those which, like that of the printers, are not intimately concerned in any productive process, are consequently outside the central struggle, and, while feeling the discomforts of change, do not feel its need.

The opposition inside the productive Trades Unions is of two kinds. There is the opposition, which is of merely psychological interest, of old Trades Union leaders who have always thought of themselves as in opposition to the Government, and feel themselves like watches without mainsprings in their new rôle of Government supporters. These are men in whom a natural intellectual stiffness makes difficult the complete change of front which was the logical result of the revolution for which they had been working. But beside that there is a much more interesting opposition based on political considerations. The Menshevik standpoint is one of disbelief in the permanence of the revolution, or rather in the permanence of the victory of the town workers. They point to the divergence in interests between the town and country populations, and are convinced that sooner or later the peasants will alter the government to suit themselves, when, once more, it will be a government against which the town workers will have to defend their interests. The Mensheviks object to the identification of the Trades Unions with the Government apparatus on the ground that when this change which they expect comes about, the Trade Union movement will be so far emasculated as to be incapable of defending the town workers against the peasants who will then be the ruling class. Thus they attack the present Trades Union leaders for being directly influenced by the Government in fixing the rate of wages, on the ground ·that this establishes a precedent from which, when the change comes, it will be difficult to break away. The Communists answer them by insisting that it is to everybody's interest to pull Russia through the crisis, and that if the Trades Unions were for such academic reasons to insist on their complete independence instead of in every possible way collaborating with the Government, they would be not only increasing the difficulties of the revolution in its economic crisis, but actually hastening that change which the Mensheviks, though they regard it as inevitable, cannot be supposed to desire. This Menshevik opposition is strongest in the Ukraine. Its strength may be judged from the figures of the Congress in Moscow this spring, when, of 1,300 delegates, over 1,000 were Communists or sympathizers with them; 63 were Mensheviks and 200 were non-party, the bulk of whom, I fancy, on this point would agree with the Mensheviks.

But apart from opposition to the "statification" of the Trades Unions, there is a cleavage cutting across the Communist Party itself and uniting in opinion, though not in voting, the Mensheviks and a section of their Communist opponents. This cleavage is over the question of "workers' control." Most of those who, before the revolution, looked forward to the "workers' control," thought of it as meaning that the actual workers in a given factory would themselves control that factory, just as a board of directors controls a factory under the ordinary capitalist system. The Communists, I think, even to-day admit the ultimate desirability of this, but insist that the important question is not who shall give the orders, but in whose interest the orders shall be given. I have nowhere found this matter properly thrashed out, though feeling upon it is extremely strong. Everybody whom I asked about it began at once to address me as if I were a public meeting, so that I found it extremely difficult to get from either side a statement not free from electioneering bias. I think, however, that it may be fairly said that all but a few lunatics have abandoned the ideas of 1917, which resulted in the workmen in a factory deposing any technical expert or manager whose orders were in the least irksome to them. These ideas and the miseries and unfairness they caused, the stoppages of work, the managers sewn up in sacks, ducked in ponds and trundled in wheelbarrows, have taken their places as curiosities of history. The change in these ideas has been gradual. The first step was the recognition that the State as a whole was interested in the efficiency of each factory, and, therefore, that the workmen of each factory had no right to arrange things with no thought except for themselves. The Committee idea was still strong, and the difficulty was got over by assuring that the technical staff should be represented on the Committee, and that the casting vote between workers and technical experts or managers should belong to the central economic organ of the State. The next stage was when the management of a workshop was given a so-called "collegiate" character, the workmen appointing representatives to share the responsibility of the "bourgeois specialist." The bitter controversy now going on concerns the seemingly inevitable transition to a later stage in which, for all practical purposes, the bourgeois specialist will be responsible solely to the State. Many Communists, including some of the best known, while recognizing the need of greater efficiency if the revolution is to survive at all, regard this step as definitely retrograde and likely in the long run to make the revolution not worth preserving.[1] The enormous importance attached by everybody to this question of individual or collegiate control, may be judged from the fact that at every conference I attended, and every discussion to which I listened, this point, which might seem of minor importance, completely overshadowed the question of industrial conscription which, at least inside the Communist Party, seemed generally taken for granted. It may be taken now as

[1] Thus Rykov, President of the Supreme Council of Public Economy: "There is a possibility of so constructing a State that in it there will be a ruling caste consisting chiefly of administrative engineers, technicians, etc.; that is, we should get a form of State economy based on a small group of a ruling caste whose privilege in this case would be the management of the workers and peasants." That criticism of individual control, from a communist, goes a good deal further than most of the criticism from people avowedly in opposition.

certain that the majority of the Communists are in favor of individual control. They say that the object of "workers' control" before the revolution was to ensure that factories should be run in the interests of workers as well of employers. In Russia now there are no employers other than the State as a whole, which is exclusively made up of employees. (I am stating now the view of the majority at the last Trades Union Congress at which I was present, April, 1920.) They say that "workers' control" exists in a larger and more efficient manner than was suggested by the old pre-revolutionary statements on that question. Further, they say that if workers' control ought to be identified with Trade Union control, the Trades Unions are certainly supreme in all those matters with which they have chiefly concerned themselves, since they dominate the Commissariat of Labor, are very largely represented on the Supreme Council of Public Economy, and fix the rates of pay for their own members.[1]

[1] The wages of workmen are decided by the Trades Unions, who draw up "tariffs" for the whole country, basing their calculations on three criteria: (1) The price of food in the open market in the district where a workman is employed, (2) the price of food supplied by the State on the card system,

The enormous Communist majority, together with the fact that however much they may quarrel with each other inside the party, the Communists will go to almost any length to avoid breaking the party discipline, means that at present the resolutions of Trades Union Congresses will not be different from those of Communist Congresses on the same subjects. Consequently, the questions which really agitate the members, the actual cleavages inside that Communist majority, are comparatively invisible at a Trades Union Congress. They are fought over with great bitterness, but they are not fought over in the Hall of the Unions—once the Club of the Nobility, with on its walls on Congress days the hammer and spanner of the engineers, the pestle and trowel of the builders, and so on—but in the Communist Congresses in the Kremlin and throughout the country. And, in the problem with which in this book we are mainly concerned, neither the regular business of the Unions nor their internal squabbles affects the cardinal fact

(3) the quality of the workman. This last is decided by a special section of the Factory Committee, which in each factory is an organ of the Trades Unions.

that in the present crisis the Trades Unions are chiefly important as part of that organization of human will with which the Communists are attempting to arrest the steady progress of Russia's economic ruin. Putting it brutally, so as to offend Trades Unionists and Communists alike, they are an important part of the Communist system of internal propaganda, and their whole organization acts as a gigantic megaphone through which the Communist Party makes known its fears, its hopes and its decisions to the great masses of the industrial workers.

THE PROPAGANDA TRAINS

WHEN I crossed the Russian front in October, 1919, the first thing I noticed in peasants' cottages, in the villages, in the little town where I took the railway to Moscow, in every railway station along the line, was the elaborate pictorial propaganda concerned with the war. There were posters showing Deniken standing straddle over Russia's coal, while the factory chimneys were smokeless and the engines idle in the yards, with the simplest wording to show why it was necessary to beat Deniken in order to get coal; there were posters illustrating the treatment of the peasants by the Whites; posters against desertion; posters illustrating the Russian struggle against the rest of the world, showing a workman, a peasant, a sailor and a soldier fighting in self-defence against an enormous Capitalistic Hydra. There were also—and this I took as a sign of what might be—posters encouraging the sowing of corn, and posters explaining in simple pictures improved methods of agriculture. Our own recruiting propaganda during the war, good as that was, was never developed to such a point of excellence, and knowing the general slowness with which the Russian centre reacts on its periphery, I was amazed not only at the actual posters, but at their efficient distribution thus far from Moscow.

I have had an opportunity of seeing two of the propaganda trains, the object of which is to reduce the size of Russia politically by bringing Moscow to the front and to the out-of-the-way districts, and so to lessen the difficulty of obtaining that general unity of purpose which it is the object of propaganda to produce. The fact that there is some hope that in the near future the whole of this apparatus may be turned over to the propaganda of industry makes it perhaps worth while to describe these trains in detail.

Russia, for purposes of this internal propaganda, is divided into five sections, and each section has its own train, prepared for the particular political needs of the section it serves, bearing its own name, carrying its regular crew—a propaganda unit, as corporate as the crew of a ship. The five trains at present in existence are the "Lenin," the "Sverdlov," the "October Revolution," the "Red East," which is now in Turkestan, and the "Red Cossack," which, ready to start for Rostov and the Don, was standing in the sidings at the Kursk station, together with the "Lenin," returned for refitting and painting.

Burov, the organizer of these trains, a ruddy, enthusiastic little man in patched leather coat and breeches, took a party of foreigners—a Swede, a Norwegian, two Czechs, a German and myself—to visit his trains, together with Radek, in the hope that Radek would induce Lenin to visit them, in which case Lenin would be kinematographed for the delight of the villagers, and possibly the Central Committee would, if Lenin were interested, lend them more lively support.

We walked along the "Lenin" first, at Burov's special request. Burov, it seems, has only recently escaped from what he considered a bitter affliction due to the Department of Proletarian Culture, who, in the beginning, for the decoration of his trains, had delivered him bound hand

and foot to a number of Futurists. For that reason he wanted us to see the "Lenin" first, in order that we might compare it with the result of his emancipation, the "Red Cossack," painted when the artists "had been brought under proper control." The "Lenin" had been painted a year and a half ago, when, as fading hoarding in the streets of Moscow still testify, revolutionary art was dominated by the Futurist movement. Every carriage is decorated with most striking but not very comprehensible pictures in the brightest colors, and the proletariat was called upon to enjoy what the pre-revolutionary artistic public had for the most part failed to understand. Its pictures are "art for art's sake," and cannot have done more than astonish, and perhaps terrify, the peasants and the workmen of the country towns who had the luck to see them. The "Red Cossack" is quite different. As Burov put it with deep satisfaction, "At first we were in the artists' hands, and now the artists are in our hands," a sentence suggesting the most horrible possibilities of official art under socialism, although, of course, bad art flourishes pretty well even under other systems.

I inquired exactly how Burov and his friends kept the artists in the right way, and received the fullest explanation. The political section of the organization works out the main idea and aim for each picture, which covers the whole side of a wagon. This idea is then submitted to a "collective" of artists, who are jointly responsible for its realization in paint. The artists compete with each other for a prize which is awarded for the best design, the judges being the artists themselves. It is the art of the poster, art with a purpose of the most definite kind. The result is sometimes amusing, interesting, startling, but, whatever else it does, hammers home a plain idea.

Thus the picture on the side of one wagon is divided into two sections. On the left is a representation of the peasants and workmen of the Soviet Republic. Under it are the words, "Let us not find ourselves again . . ." and then, in gigantic lettering under the right-hand section of the picture, ". . . in the HEAVEN OF THE WHITES." This heaven is shown by an epauletted officer hitting a soldier in the face, as was done in the Tsar's army and in at least one army of the counter revolutionaries, and workmen tied to stakes, as was done by the Whites in certain towns in the south. Then another wagon illustrating the methods of Tsardom, with a State vodka shop selling its wares to wretched folk, who, when drunk on the State vodka, are flogged by the State police. Then there is a wagon showing the different Cossacks—of the Don, Terek, Kuban, Ural—riding in pairs. The Cossack infantry is represented on the other side of this wagon. On another wagon is a very jolly picture of Stenka Razin in his boat with little old-fashioned brass cannon, rowing up the river. Underneath is written the words: "I attack only the rich, with the poor I divide everything." On one side are the poor folk running from their huts to join him, on the other the rich folk firing at him from their castle. One wagon is treated purely decoratively, with a broad effective characteristically South Russian design, framing a huge inscription to the effect that the Cossacks need not fear that the Soviet Republic will interfere with their religion, since under its régime every man is to be free to believe exactly what he likes. Then there is an entertaining wagon, showing Kolchak sitting inside a fence in Siberia

113

with a Red soldier on guard, Judenitch sitting in a little circle with a sign-post to show it is Esthonia, and Denikin running at full speed to the asylum indicated by another sign-post on which is the crescent of the Turkish Empire. Another lively picture shows the young Cossack girls learning to read, with a most realistic old Cossack woman telling them they had better not. But there is no point in describing every wagon. There are sixteen wagons in the "Red Cossack," and every one is painted all over on both sides.

The internal arrangements of the train are a sufficient proof that Russians are capable of organization if they set their minds to it. We went through it, wagon by wagon. One wagon contains a wireless telegraphy station capable of receiving news from such distant stations as those of Carnarvon or Lyons. Another is fitted up as a newspaper office, with a mechanical press capable of printing an edition of fifteen thousand daily, so that the district served by the train, however out of the way, gets its news simultaneously with Moscow, many days sometimes before the belated *Izvestia* or *Pravda* finds its way to them. And with its latest news it gets its latest propaganda, and in order to get the one it cannot help getting the other. Next door to that there is a kinematograph wagon, with benches to seat about one hundred and fifty persons. But indoor performances are only given to children, who must come during the daytime, or in summer when the evenings are too light to permit an open-air performance. In the ordinary way, at night, a great screen is fixed up in the open. There is a special hole cut in the side of the wagon, and through this the kinematograph throws its picture on the great screen outside, so that several thousands can see it at once. The enthusiastic Burov insisted on working through a couple of films for us, showing the Communist boy scouts in their country camps, children's meetings in Petrograd, and the big demonstrations of last year in honor of the Third International. He was extremely disappointed that Radek, being in a hurry, refused to wait for a performance of "The Father and his Son," a drama which, he assured us with tears in his eyes, was so thrilling that we should not regret being late for our appointments if we stayed to witness it. Another wagon is fitted up as an electric power-station, lighting the train, working the kinematograph and the printing machine, etc. Then there is a clean little kitchen and dining-room, where, before being kinematographed—a horrible experience when one is first quite seriously begged (of course by Burov) to assume an expression of intelligent interest—we had soup, a plate of meat and cabbage, and tea. Then there is a wagon bookshop, where, while customers buy books, a gramophone sings the revolutionary songs of Demian Biedny, or speaks with the eloquence of Trotsky or the logic of Lenin. Other wagons are the living-rooms of the personnel, divided up according to their duties— political, military, instructional, and so forth. For the train has not merely an agitational purpose. It carries with it a staff to give advice to local authorities, to explain what has not been understood, and so in every way to bring the ideas of the Centre quickly to the backwoods of the Republic. It works also in the opposite direction, helping to make the voice of the backwoods heard at Moscow. This is illustrated by a painted pillar-box on one of the wagons, with a slot for letters, labelled, "For Complaints of Every Kind." Anybody anywhere who has a grievance, thinks he is being unfairly treated, or has a suggestion to make, can speak with the Centre in this way. When the train is on a voyage telegrams announce its arrival beforehand, so that the local Soviets can make full use of its advantages, arranging meetings, kinematograph shows, lectures. It arrives, this amazing picture-train, and proceeds to publish and distribute its newspapers, sell its books (the bookshop, they tell me, is literally stormed at every stopping-place), send books and posters for forty versts on either side of the line with the motor-cars which it carries with it, and enliven the population with its kinematograph.

I doubt if a more effective instrument of propaganda has ever been devised. And in considering the question whether or no the Russians will be able after organizing their military defence to tackle with similar comparative success the much more difficult problem of industrial rebirth, the existence of such instruments, the use of such propaganda is a factor not to be neglected. In the spring of this year, when the civil war seemed to be ending, when there was a general belief that the Poles would accept the peace that Russia offered (they ignored this offer, advanced, took Kiev, were driven back to Warsaw, advanced again, and finally agreed to terms which they could have had in March without bloodshed of any kind), two of these propaganda trains were already being repainted with a new purpose. It was hoped that in the near future all five trains would be explaining not the need to fight but the need to work. Undoubtedly, at the first possible moment, the whole machinery of agitation, of posters, of broadsheets and of trains, will be turned over to the task of explaining the Government's plans for reconstruction, and the need for extraordinary concentration, now on transport, now on something else, that these plans involve.

SATURDAYINGS

So much for the organization, with its Communist Party, its system of meetings and counter-meetings, its adapted Trades Unions, its infinitely various propaganda, which is doing its best to make headway against ruin. I want now to describe, however briefly, the methods it has adopted in tackling the worst of all Russia's problems—the non-productivity and absolute shortage of labor.

I find a sort of analogy between these methods and those which we used in England in tackling the similar cumulative problem of finding men for war. Just as we did not proceed at once to conscription, but began by a great propaganda of voluntary effort, so the Communists, faced with a need at least equally vital, did not turn at once to industrial conscription. It was understood from the beginning that the Communists themselves were to set an example of hard work, and I dare say a considerable proportion of them did so. Every factory had its little Communist Committee, which was supposed to leaven the factory with enthusiasm, just as similar groups of Communists drafted into the armies in moments of extreme danger did, on more than one occasion, as the non-Communist Commander-in-Chief admits, turn a rout into a stand and snatch victory from what looked perilously like defeat. But this was not enough, arrears of work accumulated, enthusiasm waned, productivity decreased, and some new move was obviously necessary. This first move in the direction of industrial conscription, although no one perceived its tendency at the time, was the inauguration of what have become known as "Saturdayings."

Early in 1919 the Central Committee of the Communist Party put out a circular letter, calling upon the Communists "to work revolutionally," to emulate in the rear the heroism of their brothers on the front, pointing out that nothing but the most determined efforts and an increase in the productivity of labor would enable Russia to win through her difficulties of transport, etc. Kolchak, to quote from English newspapers, was "sweeping on to Moscow," and the situation was pretty threatening. As a direct result of this letter, on May 7th, a meeting of Communists in the sub-district of the Moscow-Kazan railway passed a resolution that, in view of the imminent danger to the Republic, Communists and their sympathizers should give up an hour a day of their leisure, and, lumping these hours together, do every Saturday six hours of manual labor; and, further, that these Communist "Saturdayings" should be continued "until complete victory over Kolchak should be assured." That decision of a local committee was the actual beginning of a movement which spread all over Russia, and though the complete victory over Kolchak was long ago obtained, is likely to continue so long as Soviet Russia is threatened by any one else.

The decision was put into effect on May 10th, when the first Communist "Saturdaying" in Russia took place on the Moscow-Kazan railway. The Commissar of the railway, Communist clerks from the offices, and every one else who wished to help, marched to work, 182 in all, and put in 1,012 hours of manual labor, in which they finished the repairs of four locomotives and sixteen wagons and loaded and unloaded 9,300 poods of engine and wagon parts and material. It was found that the productivity of labor in loading and unloading shown on this occasion was about 270 per cent. of the normal, and a similar superiority of effort was shown in the other kinds of work. This example was immediately copied on other railways. The Alexandrovsk railway had its first "Saturdaying" on May 17th. Ninety-eight persons worked for five hours, and here also did two or three times as much as the usual amount of work done in the same number of working hours under ordinary circumstances. One of the workmen, in giving an account of the performance, wrote: "The Comrades explain this by saying that in ordinary times the work was dull and they were sick of it, whereas on this occasion they were working willingly and with excitement. But now it will be shameful in ordinary hours to do less than in the Communist 'Saturdaying.'" The hope implied in this last sentence has not been realized.

In *Pravda* of June 7th there is an article describing one of these early "Saturdayings," which gives a clear picture of the infectious character of the proceedings, telling how people who came out of curiosity to look on found themselves joining in the work, and how a soldier with an accordion, after staring for a long time open-mouthed at these lunatics working on a Saturday afternoon, put up a tune for them on his instrument, and, delighted by their delight, played on while the workers all sang together.

The idea of the "Saturdayings" spread quickly from railways to factories, and by the middle of the summer reports of similar efforts were coming from all over Russia. Then Lenin became interested, seeing in these "Saturdayings" not only a special effort in the face of common danger, but an actual beginning of Communism and a sign that Socialism could bring about a greater productivity of labor than could be obtained under Capitalism. He wrote: "This is a work of great difficulty and requiring much time, but it has begun, and that is the main thing. If in hungry Moscow in the summer of 1919 hungry workmen who have lived through the difficult four years of the Imperialistic war, and then the year and a half of the still more difficult civil war, have been able to begin this great work, what will not be its further development when we conquer in the civil war and win peace." He sees in it a promise of work being done not for the sake of individual gain, but because of a recognition that such work is necessary for the general good, and in all he wrote and spoke about it he emphasized the fact that people worked better and harder when working thus than under any of the conditions (piece-work, premiums for good work, etc.) imposed by the revolution in its desperate attempts to raise the productivity of labor. For this reason alone, he wrote, the first "Saturdaying" on the Moscow-Kazan railway was an event of historical significance, and not for Russia alone.

Whether Lenin was right or wrong in so thinking, "Saturdayings" became a regular institution, like Dorcas meetings in Victorian England, like the thousands of collective working parties instituted in England during the war with Germany. It remains to be seen how long they will continue, and if they will survive peace when that comes. At present the most interesting point about them is the large proportion of non-Communists who take an enthusiastic part in them. In many cases not more than ten per cent. of Communists are concerned, though they take the iniative in organizing the parties and in finding the work to be done. The movement spread like fire in dry grass, like the craze for roller-skating swept over England some years ago, and efforts were made to control it, so that the fullest use might be made of it. In Moscow it was found worth while to set up a special Bureau for "Saturdayings." Hospitals, railways, factories, or any other concerns working for the public good, notify this bureau that they need the sort of work a "Saturdaying" provides. The bureau informs the local Communists where their services are required, and thus there is a minimum of wasted energy. The local Communists arrange the "Saturdayings," and any one else joins in who wants. These "Saturdayings" are a hardship to none because they are voluntary, except for members of the Communist Party, who are considered to have broken the party discipline if they refrain. But they can avoid the "Saturdayings" if they wish to by leaving the party. Indeed, Lenin points out that the "Saturdayings" are likely to assist in clearing out of the party those elements which joined it with the hope of personal gain. He points out that the privileges of a Communist now consist in doing more work than other people in the rear, and, on the front, in having the certainty of being killed when other folk are merely taken prisoners.

The following are a few examples of the sort of work done in the "Saturdayings." Briansk hospitals were improperly heated because of lack of the local transport necessary to bring them wood. The Communists organized a "Saturdaying," in which 900 persons took part, including military specialists (officers of the old army serving in the new), soldiers, a chief of staff, workmen and women. Having no horses, they harnessed themselves to sledges in groups of ten and brought in the wood required. At Nijni 800 persons spent their Saturday afternoon in unloading barges. In the Basman district of Moscow there was a gigantic "Saturdaying" and "Sundaying," in which 2,000 persons (in this case all but a little over 500 being Communists) worked in the heavy artillery shops, shifting materials, cleaning tramlines for bringing in fuel, etc. Then there was a "Saturdaying" the main object of which was a general autumn cleaning of the hospitals for the wounded. One form of "Saturdaying" for women is going to the hospitals, talking with the wounded and writing letters for them, mending their clothes, washing sheets, etc. The majority of "Saturdayings" at present are concerned with transport work and with getting and shifting wood, because at the moment these are the chief difficulties. I have talked to many "Saturdayers," Communist and non-Communist, and all alike spoke of these Saturday afternoons as of a kind of picnic. On the other hand, I have met Communists who were accustomed to use every kind of ingenuity to find excuses not to take part in them and yet to preserve the good opinion of their local committee.

But even if the whole of the Communist Party did actually indulge in a working picnic once a week, it would not suffice to meet Russia's tremendous needs. And, as I pointed out in the chapter specially devoted to the shortage of labor, the most serious need at present is to keep

127

skilled workers at their jobs instead of letting them drift away into non-productive labor. No amount of Saturday picnics could do that, and it was obvious long ago that some other means would have to be devised.

INDUSTRIAL CONSCRIPTION

THE general principle of industrial conscription is recognized by the Russian Constitution, section ii, chapter v, paragraph 18, which reads: "The Russian Socialist Federate Soviet Republic recognizes that work is an obligation on every citizen of the Republic," and proclaims, "He who does not work shall not eat." It is, however, one thing to proclaim such a principle and quite another to put it into action.

On December 17, 1919, the moment it became clear that there was a real possibility that the civil war was drawing to an end, Trotsky allowed the *Pravda* to print a memorandum of his, consisting of "theses" or reasoned notes about industrial conscription and the militia system. He points out that a Socialist State demands a general plan for the utilization of all the resources of a country, including its human energy. At the same time, "in the present economic chaos in

129

which are mingled the broken fragments of the
past and the beginnings of the future," a sudden
jump to a complete contralized economy of the
country as a whole is impossible. Local initiative, local effort must not be sacrificed for the
sake of a plan. At the same time industrial conscription is necessary for complete socialization.
It cannot be regardless of individuality like military conscription. He suggests a subdivision of
the State into territorial productive districts which
should coincide with the territorial districts of the
militia system which shall replace the regular
army. Registration of labor necessary. Necessary also to coördinate military and industrial
registration. At demobilization the cadres of
regiments, divisions, etc., should form the fundamental cadres of the militia. Instruction to this
end should be included in the courses for workers
and peasants who are training to become officers
in every district. Transition to the militia system must be carefully and gradually accomplished
so as not for a moment to leave the Republic de-
fenseless. While not losing sight of these ultimate aims, it is necessary to decide on immediate
needs and to ascertain exactly what amount of

labor is necessary for their limited realization. He suggests the registration of skilled labor in the army. He suggests that a Commission under the general direction of the Council of Public Economy should work out a preliminary plan and then hand it over to the War Department, so that means should be worked out for using the military apparatus for this new industrial purpose.

Trotsky's twenty-four theses or notes must have been written in odd moments, now here now there, on the way from one front to another. They do not form a connected whole. Contradictions jostle each other, and it is quite clear that Trotsky himself had no very definite plan in his head. But his notes annoyed and stimulated so many other people that they did perhaps precisely the work they were intended to do. *Pravda* printed them with a note from the editor inviting discussion. The *Ekonomitcheskaya Jizn* printed letter after letter from workmen, officials and others, attacking, approving and bringing new suggestions. Larin, Semashko, Pyatakov, Bucharin all took a hand in the discussion. Larin saw in the proposals the beginning of the end of

131

the revolution, being convinced that authority would pass from the democracy of the workers into the hands of the specialists. Rykov fell upon them with sturdy blows on behalf of the Trades Unions. All, however, agreed on the one point—that something of the sort was necessary. On December 27th a Commission for studying the question of industrial conscription was formed under the presidency of Trotsky. This Commission included the People's Commissars, or Ministers, of Labor, Ways of Communication, Supply, Agriculture, War, and the Presidents of the Central Council of the Trades Unions and of the Supreme Council of Public Economy. They compiled a list of the principal questions before them, and invited anybody interested to bring them suggestions and material for discussion.

But the discussion was not limited to the newspapers or to this Commission. The question was discussed in Soviets and Conferences of every kind all over the country. Thus, on January 1st an All-Russian Conference of local "departments for the registration and distribution of labor," after prolonged argument, contributed their views. They pointed out (1) the need of bringing to work numbers of persons who instead of doing the skilled labor for which they were qualified were engaged in petty profiteering, etc.; (2) that the evaporation of skilled labor into unproductive speculation could at least be checked by the introduction of labor books, which would give some sort of registration of each citizen's work; (3) that workmen can be brought back from the villages only for enterprises which are supplied with provisions or are situated in districts where there is plenty. ("The opinion that, in the absence of these preliminary conditions, it will be possible to draw workmen from the villages by measures of compulsion or mobilization is profoundly mistaken.") (4) that there should be a census of labor and that the Trades Unions should be invited to protect the interests of the conscripted. Finally, this Conference approved the idea of using the already existing military organization for carrying out a labor census of the Red Army, and for the turning over to labor of parts of the army during demobilization, but opposed the idea of giving the military organization the work of labor registration and industrial conscription in general.

On January 22, 1920, the Central Committee of the Communist Party, after prolonged discussion of Trotsky's rough memorandum, finally adopted and published a new edition of the "theses," expanded, altered, almost unrecognizable, a reasoned body of theory entirely different from the bundle of arrows loosed at a venture by Trotsky. They definitely accepted the principle of industrial conscription, pointing out the immediate reasons for it in the fact that Russia cannot look for much help from without and must somehow or other help herself.

Long before the All-Russian Congress of the Communist Party approved the theses of the Committee, one form of industrial conscription was already being tested at work. Very early in January, when the discussion on the subject was at its height, the Soviet of the Third Army addressed itself to the Council of Defense of the Republic with an invitation to make use of this army (which at least for the moment had finished its military task) and to experiment with it as a labor army. The Council of Defense agreed. Representatives of the Commissariats of Supply, Agriculture, Ways and Communications, Labor, and the Supreme Council of Public Economy were sent to assist the Army Soviet. The army was proudly re-named "The First Revolutionary Army of Labor," and began to issue *communiqués* "from the Labor front," precisely like the *communiqués* of an army in the field. I translate as a curiosity the first *communiqué* issued by a Labor Army's Soviet:

"Wood prepared in the districts of Ishim, Karatulskaya, Omutinskaya, Zavodoutovskaya, Yalutorovska, Iushaly, Kamuishlovo, Turinsk, Altynai, Oshtchenkovo, Shadrinsk, 10,180 cubic sazhins. Working days, 52,651. Taken to the railway stations, 5,334 cubic sazhins. Working days on transport, 22,840. One hundred carpenters detailed for the Kizelovsk mines. One hundred carpenters detailed for the bridge at Ufa. One engineer specialist detailed to the Government Council of Public Economy for repairing the mills of Chelyabinsk Government. One instructor accountant detailed for auditing the accounts of the economic organizations of Kamuishlov. Repair of locomotives proceeding in the works at Ekaterinburg. January 20, 1920, midnight."

The Labor Army's Soviet received a report on the state of the district covered by the army with regard to supply and needed work. By the end of January it had already carried out a labor census of the army, and found that it included over 50,000 laborers, of whom a considerable number were skilled. It decided on a general plan of work in reëstablishing industry in the Urals, which suffered severely during the Kolchak régime and the ebb and flow of the civil war, and was considering a suggestion of one of its members that if the scheme worked well the army should be increased to 300,000 men by way of mobilization.

On January 23rd the Council of Defense of the Republic, encouraged to proceed further, decided to make use of the Reserve Army for the improvement of railway transport on the Moscow-Kazan railway, one of the chief arteries between the eastern food districts and Moscow. The main object is to be the reëstablishment of through traffic between Moscow and Ekaterinburg and the repair of the Kazan-Ekaterinburg line, which particularly suffered during the war. An attempt was to be made to rebuild the bridge over the Kama

River before the ice melts. The Commander of the Reserve Army was appointed Commissar of the eastern part of the Moscow-Kazan railway, retaining his position as Commander of the Army. With a view of coördination between the Army Soviet and the railway authorities, a member of the Soviet was also appointed Commissar of the railway. On January 25th it was announced that a similar experiment was being made in the Ukraine. A month before the ice broke the first train actually crossed the Kama River by the rebuilt bridge.

By April of this year the organization of industrial conscription had gone far beyond the original labor armies. A decree of February 5th had created a Chief Labor Committee, consisting of five members, Serebryakov and Danilov, from the Commissariat of War; Vasiliev, from the Commissariat of the Interior; Anikst, from the Commissariat of Labor; Dzerzhinsky, from the Commissariat of Internal Affairs. Dzerzhinsky was President, and his appointment was possibly made in the hope that the reputation he had won as President of the Extraordinary Committee for Fighting Counter-Revolution would frighten people into taking this Committee seriously. Throughout the country in each government or province similar committees, called "Troikas," were created, each of three members, one from the Commissariat of War, one from the Department of Labor, one from the Department of Management, in each case from the local Commissariats and Departments attached to the local Soviet. Representatives of the Central Statistical Office and its local organs had a right to be present at the meeting of these committees of three, or "Troikas," but had not the right to vote. An organization or a factory requiring labor was to apply to the Labor Department of the local Soviet. This Department was supposed to do its best to satisfy demands upon it by voluntary methods first. If these proved insufficient they were to apply to the local "Troika," or Labor Conscription Committee. If this found that its resources also were insufficient, it was to refer back the request to the Labor Department of the Soviet, which was then to apply to its corresponding Department in the Government Soviet, which again, first voluntarily and then through the Government Committee of Labor Conscription, was

138

to try to satisfy the demands. I fancy the object of this arrangement was to prevent local "Troikas" from referring to Government "Troikas," and so directly to Dzerzhinsky's Central Committee. If they had been able to do this there would obviously have been danger lest a new network of independent and powerful organizations should be formed. Experience with the overgrown and insuppressible Committees for Fighting Counter-Revolution had taught people how serious such a development might be. Such was the main outline of the scheme for conscripting labor. A similar scheme was prepared for superintending and safeguarding labor when conscripted. In every factory of over 1,000 workmen, clerks, etc., there was formed a Commission (to distinguish it from the Committee) of Industrial Conscription. Smaller factories shared such Commissions or were joined for the purpose to larger factories near by. These Commissions were to be under the direct control of a Factory Committee, thereby preventing squabbles between conscripted and non-conscripted labor. They were to be elected for six months, but their members could be withdrawn and replaced by the Fac-

tory Committee with the approval of the local
"Troika." These Commissions, like the "Troikas," consisted of three members: (1) from the
management of the factory, (2) from the Factory
Committee, (3) from the Executive Committee
of the workers. (It was suggested in the direc-
tions that one of these should be from the group
which "has been organizing 'Saturdayings,' " that
is to say that he or she should be a Communist.)
The payment of conscripted workers was to be
by production, with prizes for specially good
work. Specially bad work was also foreseen in
the detailed scheme of possible punishments. Of-
fenders were to be brought before the "People's
Court" (equivalent to the ordinary Civil Court),
or, in the case of repeated or very bad offenses,
were to be brought before the far more dreaded
Revolutionary Tribunals. Six categories of possible offenses were placed upon the new code:

(1) Avoiding registration, absenteeism, or desertion.

(2) The preparation of false documents or the
use of such.

(3) Officials giving false information to facili-
tate these crimes.

(4) Purposeful damage of instruments or material.

(5) Uneconomical or careless work.

(6) (Probably the most serious of all) Instigation to any of these actions.

The "Troikas" have the right to deal administratively with the less important crimes by deprival of freedom for not more than two weeks. No one can be brought to trial except by the Committee for Industrial Conscription on the initiative of the responsible director of work, and with the approval either of the local labor inspection authorities or with that of the local Executive Committee.

No one with the slightest knowledge of Russia will suppose for a moment that this elaborate mechanism sprang suddenly into existence when the decree was signed. On the contrary, all stages of industrial conscription exist simultaneously even to-day, and it would be possible by going from one part of Russia to another to collect a series of specimens of industrial conscription at every stage of evolution, just as one can collect all stages of man from a baboon to a company director or a Communist. Some of the more primitive kinds of conscription were not among the least successful. For example, at the time (in the spring of this year) when the Russians still hoped that the Poles would be content with the huge area of non-Polish territory they had already seized, the army on the western front was without any elaborate system of decrees being turned into a labor army. The work done was at first ordinary country work, mainly wood-cutting. They tried to collaborate with the local "Troikas," sending help when these Committees asked for it. This, however, proved unsatisfactory, so, disregarding the "Troikas," they organized things for themselves in the whole area immediately behind the front. They divided up the forests into definite districts, and they worked these with soldiers and with deserters. Gradually their work developed, and they built themselves narrow-gauge railways for the transport of the wood. Then they needed wagons and locomotives, and of course immediately found themselves at loggerheads with the railway authorities. Finally, they struck a bargain with the railwaymen, and were allowed to take broken-down wagons which the railway people were not in a position to mend.

Using such skilled labor as they had, they mended such wagons as were given them, and later made a practice of going to the railway yards and inspecting "sick" wagons for themselves, taking out any that they thought had a chance even of temporary convalescence. Incidentally they caused great scandal by finding in the Smolensk sidings among the locomotives and wagons supposed to be sick six good locomotives and seventy perfectly healthy wagons. Then they began to improve the feeding of their army by sending the wood they had cut, in the trains they had mended, to people who wanted wood and could give them provisions. One such train went to Turkestan and back from the army near Smolensk. Their work continually increased, and since they had to remember that they were an army and not merely a sort of nomadic factory, they began themselves to mobilize, exclusively for purposes of work, sections of the civil population. I asked Unshlicht, who had much to do with this organization, if the peasants came willingly. He said, "Not very," but added that they did not mind when they found that they got well fed and were given packets of salt as prizes for good work. "The

143

peasants," he said, "do not grumble against the Government when it shows the sort of common sense that they themselves can understand. We found that when we said definitely how many carts and men a village must provide, and used them without delay for a definite purpose, they were perfectly satisfied and considered it right and proper. In every case, however, when they saw people being mobilized and sent hither and thither without obvious purpose or result, they became hostile at once." I asked Unshlicht how it was that their army still contained skilled workmen when one of the objects of industrial conscription was to get the skilled workmen back into the factories. He said: "We have an accurate census of the army, and when we get asked for skilled men for such and such a factory, they go there knowing that they still belong to the army."

That, of course, is the army point of view, and indicates one of the main squabbles which industrial conscription has produced. Trotsky would like the various armies to turn into units of a territorial militia, and at the same time to be an important part of the labor organization of each district. His opponents do not regard the labor armies as a permanent manifestation, and many have gone so far as to say that the productivity of labor in one of these armies is lower than among ordinary workmen. Both sides produce figures on this point, and Trotsky goes so far as to say that if his opponents are right, then not only are labor armies damned, but also the whole principle of industrial conscription. "If compulsory labor—independently of social conditions—is unproductive, that is a condemnation not of the labor armies, but of industrial conscription in general, and with it of the whole Soviet system, the further development of which is unthinkable except on a basis of universal industrial conscription."

But, of course, the question of the permanence of the labor armies is not so important as the question of getting the skilled workers back to the factories. The comparative success or failure of soldiers or mobilized peasants in cutting wood is quite irrelevant to this recovery of the vanished workmen. And that recovery will take time, and will be entirely useless unless it is possible to feed these workers when they have been collected. There have already been several attempts, not wholly successful, to collect the straying workers of particular industries. Thus, after the freeing of the oil-wells from the Whites, there was a general mobilization of naphtha workers. Many of these had bolted on or after the arrival of Krasnov or Denikin and gone far into Central Russia, settling where they could. So many months passed before the Red Army definitely pushed the area of civil war beyond the oil-wells, that many of these refugees had taken new root and were unwilling to return. I believe, that in spite of the mobilization, the oil-wells are still short of men. In the coal districts also, which have passed through similar experiences, the proportion of skilled to unskilled labor is very much smaller than it was before the war. There have also been two mobilizations of railway workers, and these, I think, may be partly responsible for the undoubted improvement noticeable during the year, although this is partly at least due to other things beside conscription. In the first place Trotsky carried with him into the Commissariat of Transport the same ferocious energy that he has shown in the Commissariat of War, together with the prestige that he had gained there. Further, he was well able in the councils of the Republic to defend the needs of his particular Commissariat against those of all others. He was, for example, able to persuade the Communist Party to treat the transport crisis precisely as they had treated each crisis on the front—that is to say, to mobilize great numbers of professed Communists to meet it, giving them in this case the especial task of getting engines mended and, somehow or other, of keeping trains on the move.

But neither the bridges mended and the wood cut by the labor armies, nor the improvement in transport, are any final proof of the success of industrial conscription. Industrial conscription in the proper sense of the words is impossible until a Government knows what it has to conscript. A beginning was made early this year by the introduction of labor books, showing what work people were doing and where, and serving as a kind of industrial passports. But in April this year these had not yet become general in Moscow although the less unwieldy population of Petrograd was already supplied with them. It will be long, even if it is possible at all, before any

147

considerable proportion of the people not living in these two cities are registered in this way. A more useful step was taken at the end of August, in a general census throughout Russia. There has been no Russian census since 1897. There was to have been another about the time the war began. It was postponed for obvious reasons. If the Communists carry through the census with even moderate success (they will of course have to meet every kind of evasion), they will at least get some of the information without which industrial conscription on a national scale must be little more than a farce. The census should show them where the skilled workers are. Industrial conscription should enable them to collect them and put them at their own skilled work. Then if, besides transplanting them, they are able to feed them, it will be possible to judge of the success or failure of a scheme which in most countries would bring a Government toppling to the ground.

"In most countries"; yes, but then the economic crisis has gone further in Russia than in most countries. There is talk of introducing industrial conscription (one year's service) in Germany, where things have not gone nearly so far. And perhaps industrial conscription, like Communism itself, becomes a thing of desperate hope only in a country actually face to face with ruin. I remember saying to Trotsky, when talking of possible opposition, that I, as an Englishman, with the tendencies to practical anarchism belonging to my race, should certainly object most strongly if I were mobilized and set to work in a particular factory, and might even want to work in some other factory just for the sake of not doing what I was forced to do. Trotsky replied: "You would now. But you would not if you had been through a revolution, and seen your country in such a state that only the united, concentrated effort of everybody could possibly reestablish it. That is the position here. Everybody knows the position and that there is no other way."

WHAT THE COMMUNISTS ARE TRY-ING TO DO IN RUSSIA

WE come now to the Communist plans for recon-struction. We have seen, in the first two chap-ters, something of the appalling paralysis which is the most striking factor in the economic problem to-day. We have seen how Russia is suffering from a lack of things and from a lack of labor, how these two shortages react on each other, and how nothing but a vast improvement in transport can again set in motion what was one of the great food-producing machines of the world. We have also seen something of the political organization which, with far wider ambitions before it, is at present struggling to prevent temporary paralysis from turning into permanent atrophy. We have seen that it consists of a political party so far dominant that the Trades Unions and all that is articulate in the country may be considered as part of a machinery of propaganda, for getting those things done which that political party considers should be done. In a country fighting, literally, for its life, no man can call his soul his own, and we have seen how this fact—a fact that has become obvious again and again in the history of the world, whenever a nation has had its back to the wall—is expressed in Russia in terms of industrial conscription; in measures, that is to say, which would be impossible in any country not reduced to such extremities; in measures which may prove to be the inevitable accompaniment of national crisis, when such crisis is economic rather than military. Let us now see what the Russians, with that machinery at their disposal, are trying to do.

It is obvious that since this machinery is dominated by a political party, it will be impossible to understand the Russian plans, without understanding that particular political party's estimate of the situation in general. It is obvious that the Communist plans for Russia must be largely affected by their view of Europe as a whole. This view is gloomy in the extreme. The Communists believe that Europe is steadily shaking itself to pieces. They believe that this process has already gone so far that, even given good will on the part of European Governments, the manufacturers of Western countries are already incapable of supplying them with all the things which Russia was importing before the war, still less make up the enormous arrears which have resulted from six years of blockade. They do not agree with M. Clemenceau that "revolution is a disease attacking defeated countries only." Or, to put it as I have heard it stated in Moscow, they believe that President Wilson's aspiration towards a peace in which should be neither conqueror nor conquered has been at least partially realized in the sense that every country ended the struggle economically defeated, with the possible exception of America, whose signature, after all, is still to be ratified. They believe that even in seemingly prosperous countries the seeds of economic disaster are already fertilized. They think that the demands of labor will become greater and more difficult to fulfill until at last they become incompatible with a continuance of the capitalist system. They think that strike after strike, irrespective of whether it is successful or not, will gradually widen the cracks and flaws already apparent in the damaged economic structure of Western Europe. They believe that conflicting interests will involve our nations in new national wars, and that each of these will deepen the cleavage between capital and labor. They think that even if exhaustion makes mutual warfare on a large scale impossible, these conflicting interests will produce such economic conflicts, such refusals of coöperation, as will turn exhaustion to despair. They believe, to put it briefly, that Russia has passed through the worst stages of a process to which every country in Europe will be submitted in turn by its desperate and embittered inhabitants.

We may disagree with them, but we shall not understand them if we refuse to take that belief into account. If, as they imagine, the next five years are to be years of disturbance and growing revolution, Russia will get very little from abroad. If, for example, there is to be a serious struggle in England, Russia will get practically nothing. They not only believe that these things are going to be, but make the logical deductions as to the effect of such disturbances on their own chances of importing what they need. For example, Lenin said to me that "the shock of revolution in England would ensure the final defeat of capitalism," but he said at the same time that it would be felt at once throughout the world and cause such reverberations as would paralyze industry everywhere. And that is why, although Russia is an agricultural country, the Communist plans for her reconstruction are concerned first of all not with agriculture, but with industry. In their schemes for the future of the world, Russia's part is that of a gigantic farm, but in their schemes for the immediate future of Russia, their eyes are fixed continually on the nearer object of making her so far self-supporting that, even if Western Europe is unable to help them, they may be able to crawl out of their economic difficulties, as Krassin put it to me before he left Moscow, "if necessary on all fours, but somehow or other, crawl out."

Some idea of the larger ambitions of the Communists with regard to the development of Russia are given in a conversation with Rykov, which follows this chapter. The most important characteristic of them is that they are ambitions which cannot but find an echo in Russians of any kind, quite regardless of their political convictions. The old anomalies of Russian industry, for example, the distances of the industrial districts from their sources of fuel and raw material are to be done away with. These anomalies were largely due to historical accidents, such as the caprice of Peter the Great, and not to any economic reasons. The revolution, destructive as it has been, has at least cleaned the slate and made it possible, if it is possible to rebuild at all, to rebuild Russia on foundations laid by common sense. It may be said that the Communists are merely doing flamboyantly and with a lot of flag-waving, what any other Russian Government would be doing in their place. And without the flamboyance and the flag-waving, it is doubtful whether in an exhausted country, it would be possible to get anything done at all. The result of this is that in their work of economic reconstruction the Communists get the support of most of the best engineers and other technicians in the country, men who take no interest whatsoever in the ideas of Karl Marx, but have a professional interest in doing the best they can with their knowledge, and a patriotic satisfaction in using that knowledge for Russia. These men, caring not at all about Communism, want to make Russia once more a comfortably habitable place, no matter under what Government. Their attitude is precisely comparable to that of the officers of the old army who have contributed so much to the success of the new. These officers were not Communists, but they disliked civil war, and fought to put an end of it. As Sergei Kamenev, the Commander-in-Chief, and not a Communist, said to me, "I have not looked on the civil war as on a struggle between two political ideas, for the Whites have no definite idea. I have considered it simply as a struggle between the Russian Government and a number of mutineers." Precisely so do these "bourgeois" technicians now working throughout Russia regard the task before them. It will be small satisfaction to them if famine makes the position of any Government impossible. For them the struggle is quite simply a struggle between Russia and the economic forces tending towards a complete collapse of civilization.

The Communists have thus practically the

whole intelligence of the country to help them in their task of reconstruction, or of salvage. But the educated classes alone cannot save a nation. Muscle is wanted besides brain, and the great bulk of those who can provide muscle are difficult to move to enthusiasm by any broad schemes of economic rearrangement that do not promise immediate improvement in their own material conditions. Industrial conscription cannot be enforced in Russia unless there is among the conscripted themselves an understanding, although a resentful understanding, of its necessity. The Russians have not got an army of Martians to enforce effort on an alien people. The army and the people are one. "We are bound to admit," says Trotsky, "that no wide industrial mobilization will succeed, if we do not capture all that is honorable, spiritual in the peasant working masses in explaining our plan." And the plan that he referred to was not the grandiose (but obviously sensible) plan for the eventual electrification of all Russia, but a programme of the struggle before them in actually getting their feet clear of the morass of industrial decay in which they are at present involved. Such a programme has actually been decided upon—a programme the definite object of which is to reconcile the workers to work not simply hand to mouth, each for himself, but to concentrate first on those labors which will eventually bring their reward in making other labors easier and improving the position as a whole.

Early this year a comparatively unknown Bolshevik called Gusev, to whom nobody had attributed any particular intelligence, wrote, while busy on the staff of an army on the southeast front, which was at the time being used partly as a labor army, a pamphlet which has had an extraordinary influence in getting such a programme drawn up. The pamphlet is based on Gusev's personal observation both of a labor army at work and of the attitude of the peasant towards industrial conscription. It was extremely frank, and contained so much that might have been used by hostile critics, that it was not published in the ordinary way but printed at the army press on the Caucasian front and issued exclusively to members of the Communist Party. I got hold of a copy of this pamphlet through a friend. It is called "Urgent Questions of Economic Construction." Gusev sets out in detail the sort of opposition he had met, and says: "The Anarchists, Social Revolutionaries and Mensheviks have a clear, simple economic plan which the great masses can understand: 'Go about your own business and work freely for yourself in your own place.' They have a criticism of labor mobilizations equally clear for the masses. They say to them, 'They are putting Simeon in Peter's place, and Peter in Simeon's. They are sending the men of Saratov to dig the ground in the Government of Stavropol, and the Stavropol men to the Saratov Government for the same purpose.' Then besides that there is 'non-party' criticism: 'When it is time to sow they will be shifting muck, and when it is time to reap they will be told to cut timber.' That is a particularly clear expression of the peasants' disbelief in our ability to draw up a proper economic plan. This belief is clearly at the bottom of such questions as, 'Comrade Gusev, have you ever done any plowing?' or 'Comrade Orator, do you know anything about peasant work?' Disbelief in the townsman who understands nothing about peasants is natural to the peasant, and we shall have to conquer it, to get through it, to get rid of it by showing the peasant, with a clear plan in our hands that he can understand, that we are not altogether fools in this matter and that we understand more than he does." He then sets out the argument which he himself had found successful in persuading the peasants to do things the reward for which would not be obvious the moment they were done. He says, "I compared our State economy to a colossal building with scores of stories and tens of thousands of rooms. The whole building has been half smashed; in places the roof has tumbled down, the beams have rotted, the ceilings are tumbling, the drains and water pipes are burst; the stoves are falling to pieces, the partitions are shattered, and, finally, the walls and foundations are unsafe and the whole building is threatened with collapse. I asked, how must one set about the repair of this building? With what kind of economic plan? To this question the inhabitants of different stories, and even of different rooms on one and the same story, will reply variously. Those who live on the top floor will shout that the rafters are rotten and the roof falling; that it is impossible to live there any longer, and that it is immediately necessary, first of all, to put up new beams and to repair the roof. And from their point of view they will be perfectly right. Certainly it is not possible to live any longer on that floor. Certainly the repair of the roof is necessary. The inhabitants of one of the lower stories in which the water pipes have burst will cry out that it is impossible to live without water, and therefore, first of all, the water pipes must be mended. And they, from their point of view, will be perfectly right, since it certainly is impossible to live without water. The inhabitants of the floor where the stoves have fallen to pieces will insist on an immediate mending of the stoves, since they and their children are dying of cold because there is nothing on which they can heat up water or boil *kasha* for the children; and they, too, will be quite right. But in spite of all these just demands, which arrive in thousands from all sides, it is impossible to forget the most important of all, that the foundation is shattered and that the building is threatened with a collapse which will bury all the inhabitants of the house together, and that, therefore, the *only* immediate task is the strengthening of the foundation and the walls.

161

Extraordinary firmness, extraordinary courage is necessary, not only not to listen to the cries and groans of old men, women, children and sick, coming from every floor, but also to decide on taking from the inhabitants of all floors the instruments and materials necessary for the strengthening of the foundations and walls, and to force them to leave their corners and hearths, which they are doing the best they can to make habitable, in order to drive them to work on the strengthening of the walls and foundations."

Gusev's main idea was that the Communists were asking new sacrifices from a weary and exhausted people, that without such sacrifices these people would presently find themselves in even worse conditions, and that, to persuade them to make the effort necessary to save themselves, it was necessary to have a perfectly clear and easily understandable plan which could be dinned into the whole nation and silence the criticism of all possible opponents. Copies of his little book came to Moscow. Lenin read it and caused excruciating jealousy in the minds of several other Communists, who had also been trying to find the philosopher's stone that should turn discouragement into hope, by singling out Gusev for his special praise and insisting that his plans should be fully discussed at the Supreme Council in the Kremlin. Trotsky followed Lenin's lead, and in the end a general programme for Russian reconstruction was drawn up, differing only slightly from that which Gusev had proposed. I give this scheme in Trotsky's words, because they are a little fuller than those of others, and knowledge of this plan will explain not only what the Communists are trying to do in Russia, but what they would like to get from us to-day and what they will want to get to-morrow. Trotsky says:—

"*The fundamental task at this moment is improvement in the condition of our transport, prevention of its further deterioration and preparation of the most elementary stores of food, raw material and fuel. The whole of the first period of our reconstruction will be completely occupied in the concentration of labor on the solution of these problems, which is a condition of further progress.*

"*The second period (it will be difficult to say now whether it will be measured in months or years, since that depends on many factors begin-*

ning with the international situation and ending with the unanimity or the lack of it in our own party) will be a period occupied in the building of machines in the interest of transport, and the getting of raw materials and provisions.

"The third period will be occupied in building machinery, with a view to the production of articles in general demand, and, finally, the fourth period will be that in which we are able to produce these articles."

Does it not occur, even to the most casual reader, that there is very little politics in that program, and that, no matter what kind of Government should be in Russia, it would have to endorse that programme word for word? I would ask any who doubt this to turn again to my first two chapters describing the nature of the economic crisis in Russia, and to remind themselves how, not only the lack of things but the lack of men, is intimately connected with the lack of transport, which keeps laborers ill fed, factories ill supplied with material, and in this way keeps the towns incapable of supplying the needs of the country, with the result that the country is most unwilling to supply the needs of the town. No

Russian Government unwilling to allow Russia to subside definitely to a lower level of civilization can do otherwise than to concentrate upon the improvement of transport. Labor in Russia must be used first of all for that, in order to increase its own productivity. And, if purchase of help from abroad is to be allowed, Russia must "control" the outflow of her limited assets, so that, by healing transport first of all, she may increase her power of making new assets. She must spend in such a way as eventually to increase her power of spending. She must prevent the frittering away of her small purse on things which, profitable to the vendor and doubtless desirable by the purchaser, satisfy only individual needs and do not raise the producing power of the community as a whole.

RYKOV ON ECONOMIC PLANS AND ON THE TRANSFORMATION OF THE COMMUNIST PARTY

ALEXEI RYKOV, the President of the Supreme Council of Public Economy, is one of the hardest worked men in Russia, and the only time I was able to have a long talk with him (although more than once he snatched moments to answer particular questions) was on a holiday, when the old Siberian Hotel, now the offices of the Council, was deserted, and I walked through empty corridors until I found the President and his secretary at work as usual.

After telling of the building of the new railway from Alexandrovsk Gai to the Emba, the prospects of developing the oil industry in that district, the relative values of those deposits and of those at Baku, and the possible decreasing significance of Baku in Russian industry generally,

166

we passed to broader perspectives. I asked him what he thought of the relations between agriculture and industry in Russia, and supposed that he did not imagine that Russia would ever become a great industrial country. His answer was characteristic of the tremendous hopes that nerve these people in their almost impossible task, and I set it down as nearly as I can in his own words. For him, of course, the economic problem was the first, and he spoke of it as the director of a huge trust might have spoken. But, as he passed on to talk of what he thought would result from the Communist method of tackling that problem, and spoke of the eventual disappearance of political parties, I felt I was trying to read a kind of palimpsest of the *Economist* and *News from Nowhere*, or listening to a strange compound of William Morris and, for example, Sir Eric Geddes. He said:—

"We may have to wait a long time before the inevitable arrives and there is a Supreme Economic Council dealing with Europe as with a single economic whole. If that should come about we should, of course, from the very nature of our country, be called upon in the first place to provide food for Europe, and we should hope enormously to improve our agriculture, working on a larger and larger scale, using mechanical plows and tractors, which would be supplied us by the West. But in the meantime we have to face the fact that events may cause us to be, for all practical purposes, in a state of blockade for perhaps a score of years, and, so far as we can, we must be ready to depend on ourselves alone. For example, we want mechanical plows which could be procured abroad. We have had to start making them ourselves. The first electric plow made in Russia and used in Russia started work last year, and this year we shall have a number of such plows made in our country, not because it is economic so to make them, but because we could get them in no other way. In so far as is possible, we shall have to make ourselves self-supporting, so as somehow or other to get along even if the blockade, formal or perhaps willy-nilly (imposed by the inability of the West to supply us), compels us to postpone coöperation with the rest of Europe. Every day of such postponement is one in which the resources of Europe are not being used in the most efficient manner to supply

168

the needs not only of our own country but of all."

I referred to what he had told me last year about the intended electrification of Moscow by a station using turf fuel.

"That," he said, "is one of the plans which, in spite of the war, has gone a very long way towards completion. We have built the station in the Ryezan Government, on the Shadul peat mosses, about 110 versts from Moscow. Before the end of May that station should be actually at work. (It was completed, opened and partially destroyed by a gigantic fire.) Another station at Kashira in the Tula Government (on the Oka), using the small coal produced in the Moscow coalfields, will be at work before the autumn. This year similar stations are being built at Ivano-Voznesensk and at Nijni-Novgorod. Also, with a view to making the most economic use of what we already possess, we have finished both in Petrograd and in Moscow a general unification of all the private power-stations, which now supply their current to a single main cable. Similar unification is nearly finished at Tula and at Kostroma. The big water-power station on the rapids of the Volkhov is finished in so far as land construction goes, but we can proceed no further until we have obtained the turbines, which we hope to get from abroad. As you know, we are basing our plans in general on the assumption that in course of time we shall supply the whole of Russian industry with electricity, of which we also hope to make great use in agriculture. That, of course, will take a great number of years."

[Nothing could have been much more artificial than the industrial geography of old Russia. The caprice of history had planted great industrial centers literally at the greatest possible distance from the sources of their raw materials. There was Moscow bringing its coal from Donetz, and Petrograd, still further away, having to eke out a living by importing coal from England. The difficulty of transport alone must have forced the Russians to consider how they could do away with such anomalies. Their main idea is that the transport of coal in a modern State is an almost inexcusable barbarism. They have set themselves, these ragged engineers, working in rooms which they can hardly keep above freezing-point and walking home through the snow in boots without soles, no less a task than the electrification of the whole of Russia. There is a State Committee presided over by an extraordinary optimist called Krzhizhanovsky, entrusted by the Supreme Council of Public Economy and Commissariat of Agriculture with the working out of a general plan. This Committee includes, besides a number of well-known practical engineers, Professors Latsinsky, Klassen, Dreier, Alexandrov, Tcharnovsky, Dend and Pavlov. They are investigating the water power available in different districts in Russia, the possibilities of using turf, and a dozen similar questions including, perhaps not the least important, investigation to discover where they can do most with least dependence on help from abroad.]

Considering the question of the import of machinery from abroad, I asked him whether in existing conditions of transport Russia was actually in a position to export the raw materials with which alone the Russians could hope to buy what they want. He said:

"Actually we have in hand about two million poods (a pood is a little over thirty-six English pounds) of flax, and any quantity of light leather (goat, etc.), but the main districts where we have raw material for ourselves or for export are far away. Hides, for example, we have in great quantities in Siberia, in the districts of Orenburg and the Ural River and in Tashkent. I have myself made the suggestion that we should offer to sell this stuff where it is, that is to say not delivered at a seaport, and that the buyers should provide their own trains, which we should eventually buy from them with the raw material itself, so that after a certain number of journeys the trains should become ours. In the same districts we have any quantity of wool, and in some of these districts corn. We cannot, in the present condition of our transport, even get this corn for ourselves. In the same way we have great quantities of rice in Turkestan, and actually are being offered rice from Sweden, because we cannot transport our own. Then we have over a million poods of copper, ready for export on the same conditions. But it is clear that if the Western countries are unable to help in the transport, they cannot expect to get raw materials from us."

I asked about platinum. He laughed.

"That is a different matter. In platinum we

have a world monopoly, and can consequently afford to wait. Diamonds and gold, they can have as much as they want of such rubbish; but platinum is different, and we are in no hurry to part with it. But diamonds and gold ornaments, the jewelry of the Tsars, we are ready to give to any king in Europe who fancies them, if he can give us some less ornamental but more useful locomotives instead."

I asked if Kolchak had damaged the platinum mines. He replied, "Not at all. On the contrary, he was promising platinum to everybody who wanted it, and he set the mines going, so we arrived to find them in good condition, with a considerable yield of platinum ready for use."

(I am inclined to think that in spite of Rykov's rather intransigent attitude on the question, the Russians would none the less be willing to export platinum, if only on account of the fact in comparison with its great value it requires little transport, and so would make possible for them an immediate bargain with some of the machinery they most urgently need.)

Finally we talked of the growing importance of the Council of Public Economy. Rykov was of opinion that it would eventually become the centre of the whole State organism, "it and the Trades Unions organizing the actual producers in each branch."

"Then you think that as your further plans develop, with the creation of more and more industrial centres, with special productive populations concentrated round them, the Councils of the Trades Unions will tend to become identical with the Soviets elected in the same districts by the same industrial units?"

"Precisely," said Rykov, "and in that way the Soviets, useful during the period of transition as an instrument of struggle and dictatorship, will be merged with the Unions." (One important factor, as Lenin pointed out when considering the same question, is here left out of count, namely the political development of the enormous agricultural as opposed to industrial population.)

"But if this merging of political Soviets with productive Unions occurs, the questions that concern people will cease to be political questions, but will be purely questions of economics."

"Certainly. And we shall see the disappearance of political parties. That process is already apparent. In the present huge Trade Union Conference there are only sixty Mensheviks. The Communists are swallowing one party after another. Those who were not drawn over to us during the period of struggle are now joining us during the process of construction, and we find that our differences now are not political at all, but concerned only with the practical details of construction." He illustrated this by pointing out the present constitution of the Supreme Council of Public Economy. There are under it fifty-three Departments or Centres (Textile, Soap, Wool, Timber, Flax, etc.), each controlled by a "College" of three or more persons. There are 232 members of these Colleges or Boards in all, and of them 83 are workmen, 79 are engineers, 1 was an ex-director, 50 were from the clerical staff, and 19 unclassified. Politically 115 were Communists, 105 were "non-party," and 12 were of non-Communist parties. He continued, "Further, in swallowing the other parties, the Communists themselves will cease to exist as a political party. Think only that youths coming to their manhood during this year in Russia and in the future will not be able to confirm from

175

their own experience the reasoning of Karl Marx, because they will have had no experience of a capitalist country. What can they make of the class struggle? The class struggle here is already over, and the distinctions of class have already gone altogether. In the old days, members of our party were men who had read, or tried to read, Marx's "Capital," who knew the "Communist Manifesto" by heart, and were occupied in continual criticism of the basis of capitalist society. Look at the new members of our party. Marx is quite unnecessary to them. They join us, not for struggle in the interests of an oppressed class, but simply because they understand our aims in constructive work. And, as this process continues, we old social democrats shall disappear, and our places will be filled by people of entirely different character grown up under entirely new conditions."

NON-PARTYISM

Rykov's prophecies of the disappearance of political parties may be falsified by a development of that very non-partyism on which he bases them. It is true that the parties openly hostile to the Communists in Russia have practically disappeared. Many old-time Mensheviks have joined the Communist Party. Here and there in the country may be found a Social Revolutionary stronghold. Here and there in the Ukraine the Mensheviks retain a footing, but I doubt whether either of these parties has in it the vitality to make itself once again a serious political factor. There is, however, a movement which, in the long run, may alter Russia's political complexion. More and more delegates to Soviets or Congresses of all kinds are explicitly described as "Non-party." Non-partyism is perhaps a sign of revolt against rigid discipline of any kind. Now

177

and then, of course, a clever Menshevik or Social
Revolutionary, by trimming his sails carefully to
the wind, gets himself elected on a non-party
ticket. When this happens there is usually a
great hullabaloo as soon as he declares himself.
A section of his electors agitates for his recall
and presently some one else is elected in his stead.
But non-partyism is much more than a mere cloak
of invisibility for enemies or conditional supporters of the Communists. I know of considerable
country districts which, in the face of every kind
of agitation, insist on returning exclusively non-
party delegates. The local Soviets in these districts are also non-party, and they elect usually
a local Bolshevik to some responsible post to act
as it were as a buffer between themselves and the
central authority. They manage local affairs in
their own way, and, through the use of tact on
both sides, avoid falling foul of the more rigid
doctrinaires in Moscow.

Eager reactionaries outside Russia will no doubt
point to non-partyism as a symptom of friendship
for themselves. It is nothing of the sort. On all
questions of the defense of the Republic the non-
party voting is invariably solid with that of the

Communists. The non-party men do not want Denikin. They do not want Baron Wrangel. They have never heard of Professor Struhve. They do not particularly like the Communists. They principally want to be left alone, and they principally fear any enforced continuation of war of any kind. If, in the course of time, they come to have a definite political programme, I think it not impossible that they may turn into a new kind of constitutional democrat. That does not mean that they will have any use for M. Milukov or for a monarch with whom M. Milukov might be ready to supply them. The Constitution for which they will work will be that very Soviet Constitution which is now in abeyance, and the democracy which they associate with it will be that form of democracy which were it to be accurately observed in the present state of Russia, that Constitution would provide. The capitalist in Russia has long ago earned the position in which, according to the Constitution, he has a right to vote, since he has long ago ceased to be a capitalist. Supposing the Soviet Constitution were to-day to be literally applied, it would be found that practically no class except the priests would be excluded from the franchise. And when this agitation swells in volume, it will be an agitation extremely difficult to resist, supposing Russia to be at peace, so that there will be no valid excuse with which to meet it. These new constitutional democrats will be in the position of saying to the Communists, "Give us, without change, that very Constitution which you yourselves drew up." I think they will find many friends inside the Communist Party, particularly among those Communists who are also Trade Unionists. I heard something very like the arguments of this new variety of constitutional democrat in the Kremlin itself at an All-Russian Conference of the Communist Party. A workman, Sapronov, turned suddenly aside in a speech on quite another matter, and said with great violence that the present system was in danger of running to seed and turning into oligarchy, if not autocracy. Until the moment when he put his listeners against him by a personal attack on Lenin, there was no doubt that he had with him the sympathies of quite a considerable section of an exclusively Communist audience.

Given peace, given an approximate return to

normal conditions, non-partyism may well profoundly modify the activities of the Communists. It would certainly be strong enough to prevent the rasher spirits among them from jeopardizing peace or from risking Russia's chance of convalescence for the sake of promoting in any way the growth of revolution abroad. Of course, so long as it is perfectly obvious that Soviet Russia is attacked, no serious growth of non-partyism is to be expected, but it is obvious that any act of aggression on the part of the Soviet Government, once Russia had attained peace—which she has not known since 1914—would provide just the basis of angry discontent which might divide even the disciplined ranks of the Communists and give non-partyism an active, instead of a comparatively passive, backing throughout the country.

Non-partyism is already the peasants' way of expressing their aloofness from the revolution and, at the same time, their readiness to defend that revolution against anybody who attacks it from outside. Lenin, talking to me about the general attitude of the peasants, said: "Hegel wrote 'What is the People? The people is that part of the nation which does not know what it wants.'

That is a good description of the Russian peasantry at the present time, and it applies equally well to your Arthur Hendersons and Sidney Webbs in England, and to all other people like yourself who want incompatible things. The peasantry are individualists, but they support us. We have, in some degree, to thank Kolchak and Denikin for that. They are in favor of the Soviet Government, but hanker after Free Trade, not understanding that the two things are self-contradictory. Of course, if they were a united political force they could swamp us, but they are disunited both in their interests and geographically. The interests of the poorer and middle-class peasants are in contradiction to those of the rich peasant farmer who employs laborers. The poorer and middle class see that we support them against the rich peasant, and also see that he is ready to support what is obviously not in their interests." I said, "If State agriculture in Russia comes to be on a larger scale, will there not be a sort of proletarianization of the peasants so that, in the long run, their interests will come to be more or less identical with those of the workers in other than agricultural industry?" He replied, "Something in that direction is being done, but it will have to be done very carefully and must take a very long time. When we are getting many thousands of tractors from abroad, then something of the sort would become possible." Finally I asked him point blank, "Did he think they would pull through far enough economically to be able to satisfy the needs of the peasantry before that same peasantry had organized a real political opposition that should overwhelm them?" Lenin laughed. "If I could answer that question," he said, "I could answer everything, for on the answer to that question everything depends. I think we can. Yes, I think we can. But I do not know that we can."

Non-partyism may well be the protoplasmic stage of the future political opposition of the peasants.

POSSIBILITIES

I HAVE done my best to indicate the essential facts in Russia's problem to-day, and to describe the organization and methods with which she is attempting its solution. I can give no opinion as to whether by these means the Russians will succeed in finding their way out of the quagmire of industrial ruin in which they are involved. I can only say that they are unlikely to find their way out by any other means. I think this is instinctively felt in Russia. Not otherwise would it have been possible for the existing organization, battling with one hand to save the towns from starvation, to destroy with the other the various forces clothed and armed by Western Europe, which have attempted its undoing. The mere fact of continued war has, of course, made progress in the solution of the economic problem almost impossible, but the fact that the economic problem was unsolved, must have made war impossible, if it were not that the instinct of the people was definitely against Russian or foreign invaders. Consider for one moment the military position.

Although the enthusiasm for the Polish war began to subside (even among the Communists) as soon as the Poles had been driven back from Kiev to their own frontiers, although the Poles are occupying an enormous area of non-Polish territory, although the Communists have had to conclude with Poland a peace obviously unstable, the military position of Soviet Russia is infinitely better this time than it was in 1918 or 1919. In 1918 the Ukraine was held by German troops and the district east of the Ukraine was in the hands of General Krasnov, the author of a flattering letter to the Kaiser. In the northwest the Germans were at Pskov, Vitebsk and Mohilev. We ourselves were at Murmansk and Archangel. In the east, the front which became known as that of Kolchak, was on the Volga. Soviet Russia was a little hungry island with every prospect of submersion. A year later the Germans had vanished, the flatterers of the Kaiser had joined hands with those who were temporarily flattering the Allies, Yudenitch's troops were within sight of Petrograd, Denikin was at Orel, almost within striking distance of Moscow; there had been a stampede of desertion from the Red Army. There was danger that Finland might strike at any moment. Although in the east Kolchak had been swept over the Urals to his ultimate disaster, the situation of Soviet Russia seemed even more desperate than in the year before. What is the position to-day? Esthonia, Latvia, Lithuania, and Finland are at peace with Russia. The Polish peace brings comparative quiet to the western front, although the Poles, keeping the letter rather than the spirit of their agreement, have given Balahovitch the opportunity of establishing himself in Minsk, where, it is said, that the pogroms of unlucky Jews show that he has learnt nothing since his ejection from Pskov.

Balahovitch's force is not important in itself, but its existence will make it easy to start the war afresh along the whole new frontier of Poland, and that frontier shuts into Poland so large an anti-Polish population, that a moment may still come when desperate Polish statesmen may again choose war as the least of many threatening evils. Still, for the moment, Russia's western frontier is comparatively quiet. Her northern frontier is again the Arctic Sea. Her eastern frontier is in the neighborhood of the Pacific. The Ukraine is disorderly, but occupied by no enemy; the only front on which serious fighting is proceeding is the small semi-circle north of the Crimea. There Denikin's successor, supported by the French but exultantly described by a German conservative newspaper as a "German baron in Cherkass uniform," is holding the Crimea and a territory slightly larger than the peninsula on the main land. Only to the immense efficiency of anti-Bolshevik propaganda can be ascribed the opinion, common in England but comic to any one who takes the trouble to look at a map, that Soviet Russia is on the eve of military collapse.

In any case it is easy in a revolution to magnify the influence of military events on internal affairs. In the first place, no one who has not actually crossed the Russian front during the period of active operations can well realize how different are the revolutionary wars from that

which ended in 1918.   Advance on a broad front
no longer means that a belt of men in touch with
each other has moved definitely forward.   It
means that there have been a series of forward
movements at widely separated, and with the very
haziest of mutual, connections.   There will be
violent fighting for a village or a railway station
or the passage of a river.   Small hostile groups
will engage in mortal combat to decide the possession of a desirable hut in which to sleep, but,
except at these rare points of actual contact, the
number of prisoners is far in excess of the number
of casualties.   Parties on each side will be perfectly ignorant of events to right or left of them,
ignorant even of their gains and losses.   Last
year I ran into Whites in a village which the Reds
had assured me was strongly held by themselves,
and these same Whites refused to believe that the
village where I had spent the preceding night was
in the possession of the Reds.   It is largely an
affair of scouting parties, of patrols dodging each
other through the forest tracks, of swift raids, of
sudden conviction (often entirely erroneous) on
the part of one side or the other, that it or the
enemy has been "encircled."   The actual num-

ber of combatants to a mile of front is infinitely less than during the German war. Further, since an immense proportion of these combatants on both sides have no wish to fight at all, being without patriotic or political convictions and very badly fed and clothed, and since it is more profitable to desert than to be taken prisoner, desertion in bulk is not uncommon, and the deserters, hurriedly enrolled to fight on the other side, indignantly re-desert when opportunity offers. In this way the armies of Denikin and Yudenitch swelled like mushrooms and decayed with similar rapidity. Military events of this kind, however spectacular they may seem abroad, do not have the political effect that might be expected. I was in Moscow at the worst moment of the crisis in 1919 when practically everybody outside the Government believed that Petrograd had already fallen, and I could not but realize that the Government was stronger then than it had been in February of the same year, when it had had a series of victories and peace with the Allies seemed for a moment to be in sight. A sort of fate seems to impel the Whites to neutralize with extraordinary rapidity any good will for themselves which they may find among the population. This is true of both sides, but seems to affect the Whites especially. Although General Baron Wrangel does indeed seem to have striven more successfully than his predecessors not to set the population against him and to preserve the loyalty of his army, it may be said with absolute certainty that any large success on his part would bring crowding to his banner the same crowd of stupid reactionary officers who brought to nothing any mild desire for moderation that may have been felt by General Denikin. If the area he controls increases, his power of control over his subordinates will decrease, and the forces that led to Denikin's collapse will be set in motion in his case also.[1] And, of course, should hostilities

[1] On the day on which I send this book to the printers news comes of Wrangel's collapse and flight. I leave standing what I have written concerning him, since it will apply to any successor he may have. Each general who has stepped into Kolchak's shoes has eventually had to run away in them, and always for the same reasons. It may be taken almost as an axiom that the history of a great country is that of its centre, not of its periphery. The main course of English history throughout the troubled seventeenth and eighteenth centuries was never deflected from London. French history did not desert Paris, to make a new start at Toulon or at Quiberon Bay. And only a fanatic could suppose that Russian history would run away from Moscow, to begin again in a semi-

flare up again on the Polish frontier, should the lions and lambs and jackals and eagles of Kossack, Russian, Ukrainian and Polish nationalists temporarily join forces, no miracles of diplomacy will keep them from coming to blows. For all these reasons a military collapse of the Soviet Government at the present time, even a concerted military advance of its enemies, is unlikely.

It is undoubtedly true that the food situation in the towns is likely to be worse this winter than it has yet been. Forcible attempts to get food from the peasantry will increase the existing hostility between town and country. There has been a very bad harvest in Russia. The bringing of food from Siberia or the Kuban (if military activities do not make that impossible) will impose

Tartar peninsula in the Black Sea. Moscow changes continually, and may so change as to make easy the return of the "refugees." Some have already returned. But the refugees will not return as conquerors. Should a Russian Napoleon (an unlikely figure, even in spite of our efforts) appear, he will not throw away the invaluable asset of a revolutionary war-cry. He will have to fight some one, or he will not be a Napoleon. And whom will he fight but the very people who, by keeping up the friction, have rubbed Aladdin's ring so hard and so long that a Djinn, by no means kindly disposed towards them, bursts forth at last to avenge the breaking of his sleep?

an almost intolerable strain on the inadequate transport. Yet I think internal collapse unlikely. It may be said almost with certainty that Governments do not collapse until there is no one left to defend them. That moment had arrived in the case of the Tsar. It had arrived in the case of Kerensky. It has not arrived in the case of the Soviet Government for certain obvious reasons. For one thing, a collapse of the Soviet Government at the present time would be disconcerting, if not disastrous, to its more respectable enemies. It would, of course, open the way to a practically unopposed military advance, but at the same time it would present its enemies with enormous territory, which would overwhelm the organizing powers which they have shown again and again to be quite inadequate to much smaller tasks. Nor would collapse of the present Government turn a bad harvest into a good one. Such a collapse would mean the breakdown of all existing organizations, and would intensify the horrors of famine for every town dweller. Consequently, though the desperation of hunger and resentment against inevitable requisitions may breed riots and revolts here and there throughout the country, the men who, in other circumstances, might co-ordinate such events, will refrain from doing anything of the sort. I do not say that collapse is impossible. I do say that it would be extremely undesirable from the point of view of almost everybody in Russia. Collapse of the present Government would mean at best a reproduction of the circumstances of 1917, with the difference that no intervention from without would be necessary to stimulate indiscriminate slaughter within. I say "at best" because I think it more likely that collapse would be followed by a period of actual chaos. Any Government that followed the Communists would be faced by the same economic problem, and would have to choose between imposing measures very like those of the Communists and allowing Russia to subside into a new area for colonization. There are people who look upon this as a natural, even a desirable, result of the revolution. They forget that the Russians have never been a subject race, that they have immense powers of passive resistance, that they respond very readily to any idea that they understand, and that the idea of revolt against foreigners is difficult not to understand. Any country that takes advantage of the Russian people in a moment of helplessness will find, sooner or later, first that it has united Russia against it, and secondly that it has given all Russians a single and undesirable view of the history of the last three years. There will not be a Russian who will not believe that the artificial incubation of civil war within the frontiers of old Russia was not deliberately undertaken by Western Europe with the object of so far weakening Russia as to make her exploitation easy. Those who look with equanimity even on this prospect forget that the creation in Europe of a new area for colonization, a knocking out of one of the sovereign nations, will create a vacuum, and that the effort to fill this vacuum will set at loggerheads nations at present friendly and so produce a struggle which may well do for Western Europe what Western Europe will have done for Russia.

It is of course possible that in some such way the Russian Revolution may prove to be no more than the last desperate gesture of a stricken civilization. My point is that if that is so, civilization in Russia will not die without infecting us with its disease. It seems to me that our own civilization is ill already, slightly demented perhaps, and liable, like a man in delirium, to do things which tend to aggravate the malady. I think that the whole of the Russian war, waged directly or indirectly by Western Europe, is an example of this sort of dementia, but I cannot help believing that sanity will reassert itself in time. At the present moment, to use a modification of Gusev's metaphor, Europe may be compared to a burning house and the Governments of Europe to fire brigades, each one engaged in trying to salve a wing or a room of the building. It seems a pity that these fire brigades should be fighting each other, and forgetting the fire in their resentment of the fact that some of them wear red uniforms and some wear blue. Any single room to which the fire gains complete control increases the danger of the whole building, and I hope that before the roof falls in the firemen will come to their senses.

But turning from grim recognition of the danger, and from speculations as to the chance of the Russian Government collapsing, and as to the changes in it that time may bring, let us consider

195

what is likely to happen supposing it does not collapse. I have already said that I think collapse unlikely. Do the Russians show any signs of being able to carry out their programme, or has the fire gone so far during the quarrelling of the firemen as to make that task impossible?

I think that there is still a hope. There is as yet no sign of a general improvement in Russia, nor is such an improvement possible until the Russians have at least carried out the first stage of their programme. It would even not be surprising if things in general were to continue to go to the bad during the carrying out of that first stage. Shortages of food, of men, of tools, of materials, are so acute that they have had to choose those factories which are absolutely indispensable for the carrying out of this stage, and make of them "shock" factories, like the "shock" troops of the war, giving them equipment over and above their rightful share of the impoverished stock, feeding their workmen even at the cost of letting others go hungry. That means that other factories suffer. No matter, say the Russians, if only that first stage makes progress. Consequently, the only test that can be fairly applied is that of transport. Are they or are they not gaining on ruin in the matter of wagons and engines? Here are the figures of wagon repairs in the seven chief repairing shops up to the month of June:

December 1919 ...	475	wagons	were	repaired.
January 1920	656	”	”	”
February ”	697	”	”	”
March ”	1,104	”	”	”
April ”	1,141	”	”	”
May ”	1,154	”	”	”
June ”	1,161	”	”	”

After elaborate investigation last year, Trotsky, as temporary Commissar of Transport, put out an order explaining that the railways, to keep up their present condition, must repair roughly 800 engines every month. During the first six months of 1920 they fulfilled this task in the following percentages:

January	32	per cent.
February	50	”
March	66	”
April	78	”
May	98	”
June	104	”

I think that is a proof that, supposing normal relations existed between Russia and ourselves, the Russian would be able to tackle the first stage of the problem that lies before them, and would lie before them whatever their Government might be. Unfortunately there is no proof that this steady improvement can be continued, except under conditions of trade with Western Europe. There are Russians who think they can pull through without us, and, remembering the miracles of which man is capable when his back is to the wall, it would be rash to say that this is impossible. But other Russians point out gloomily that they have been using certain parts taken from dead engines (engines past repair) in order to mend sick engines. They are now coming to the mending, not of sick engines merely, but of engines on which post-mortems have already been held. They are actually mending engines, parts of which have already been taken out and used for the mending of other engines. There are consequently abnormal demands for such things as shafts and piston rings. They are particularly short of Babbitt metal and boiler tubes. In normal times the average number of new tubes wanted for each engine put through the repair shops was 25 (10 to 15 for engines used in the more northerly districts, and 30 to 40 for engines in the south where the water is not so good). This number must now be taken as much higher, because during recent years tubes have not been regularly renewed. Further, the railways have been widely making use of tubes taken from dead engines, that is to say, tubes already worn. Putting things at their very best, assuming that the average demand for tubes per engine will be that of normal times, then, if 1,000 engines are to be repaired monthly, 150,000 tubes will be wanted every six months. Now on the 15th of June the total stock of tubes ready for use was 58,000, and the railways could not expect to get more than another 13,000 in the near future. Unless the factories are able to do better (and their improvement depends on improvement in transport), railway repairs must again deteriorate, since the main source of materials for it in Russia, namely the dead engines, will presently be exhausted.

On this there is only one thing to be said. If, whether because we do not trade with them, or from some other cause, the Russians are unable

to proceed even in this first stage of their programme, it means an indefinite postponement of
the moment when Russia will be able to export
anything, and, consequently, that when at last we
learn that we need Russia as a market, she will be
a market willing to receive gifts, but unable to
pay for anything at all. And that is a state of
affairs a great deal more serious to ourselves than
to the Russians, who can, after all, live by wan-
dering about their country and scratching the
ground, whereas we depend on the sale of our
manufactured goods for the possibility of buying
the food we cannot grow ourselves. If the Russians fail, their failure will affect not us alone.
It will, by depriving her of a market, lessen Germany's power of recuperation, and consequently
her power of fulfilling her engagements. What,
then, is to happen to France? And, if we are
to lose our market in Russia, and find very much
weakened markets in Germany and France, we
shall be faced with an ever-increasing burden of
unemployment, with the growth, in fact, of the
very conditions in which alone we shall ourselves
be unable to recover from the war. In such conditions, upheaval in England would be possible,

and, for the dispassionate observer, there is a strange irony in the fact that the Communists desire that upheaval, and, at the same time, desire a rebirth of the Russian market which would tend to make that upheaval unlikely, while those who most fear upheaval are precisely those who urge us, by making recovery in Russia impossible, to improve the chances of collapse at home. The peasants in Russia are not alone in wanting incompatible things.

CPSIA information can be obtained
at www.ICGtesting.com
Printed in the USA
LVHW102241080620
657704LV00008B/329

9 781276 554374